oduction

HIRE ME IF YOU CAN

HIRE ME IF YOU CAN

HIRE ME IF YOU CAN

666 dirty secrets to recruit top growth hacking talent before your competitors do

by Nader Sabry

Copyright

Printed in the United States of America and Canada.

Nader Sabry, Hire me if you can - 666 dirty secrets to recruit top growth hacking talent before your competitors do

978-1-9163569-8-6 Paperback
978-1-9163569-9-3 Hardcover

1. BUSINESS & ECONOMICS / Entrepreneurship, 2. BUSINESS & ECONOMICS / Corporate Finance / Venture Capital, 3. BUSINESS & ECONOMICS / Industries / Computers & Information Technology

First Edition, and first print in 2022-2023

Nader Sabry
Royal Oak. P.O. Box 91022
Calgary Alberta, Canada T3G 0B1

www.hiremeifyoucan.com
www.nadersabry.com
www.MyGrowthThinking.com
www.ReadySetGrowthHack.com

HIRE ME IF YOU CAN

Order your copy of
Growth Thinking Design

HIRE ME IF YOU CAN

Contents

Preface   13

About this book   16

Introduction   30

Part 1 The Talent explosion   35

Part 2 Growth hackers in demand   62

Part 3 666 dirty hacks to recruit growth hackers   74

Conclusion   279

About the author   279

Preface

After building and growing hundreds of organizations over the past 25 years, I have developed the foundation to *"The science of exponential growth"*. This science has been documented, measured and stress-tested over several full-cycle runs from start to finish.

With a comprehensive build-up of tools and resources in the space of the science of exponential growth, I started with a build print for organizations to use (in my first book, *Ready, Set, Growth Hack*). Then, I provided a design process to implement (in my second book, *Growth Thinking*), and data to support the growth experiments (presented in *Growth Labz)*. Three main lessons have been highlighted:

1. There is no single success formula; you have to create your own
2. The biggest growth opportunities come from the unknown
3. Systematically scaling only works when full-scale operation is mastered

With all of this in the backdrop, over years of building, a single question arises time and again from clients, during training, and in talks:

How do I hire a growth hacker?

The profound aspect of this question isn't what they are asking, but more interestingly, why. Once they have realized the importance of the science of exponential growth, they instantly understand that they need an expert to achieve – or help them achieve – exponential growth.

Answering this question isn't easy, as there are many moving parts. These include everything from training, development, learning, skilling, re-skilling and assessments to placements, performance, culture, and alignment. As you can imagine, this is a much deeper topic than initially imagined.

I wrote this book to shed light on the complexity of the topic, ways to manage it and to enable the reader to gain a competitive advantage as fast as possible.

This book will answer the top-level parts of this question, while offering a background to what is happening and why; finally, it will provide many practical strategies to tackle the problem.

Get ready, because the **next decade of growth is going to be challenging**, and everything that can help you – even if it gives you a one-inch advantage – will count. Welcome to the dirty recruitment secrets behind hiring a growth hacker your competitors don't want you to know about – or act on.

About this book

After working with hundreds of clients on growth, one common question kept arising. It would appear at the start of the work, during the process and even after the client's work was completed. The question was "How do I hire a growth hacker?"

This question isn't easy to answer and this is why it keeps coming up. There are also a few distinct misconceptions that need to be moved out of the way first.

1. Marketing is not growth
2. Digital marketing is not growth
3. Not everyone with the word "growth" in their job title is an expert in growth
4. Growth hacking is not illegal, unethical or immoral

An important fact to establish is that growth is a science, and it's science anyone can learn, but you currently cannot learn it in formal educational institutes. Keep that in mind, as growth hacking is a new discipline, so it is not formally taught in educational institutes. That is changing, but the key factor of success in learning this new science is that it needs to be practiced within a valid environment, where feedback is measured and results lead to learning in a structured process.

The science behind this is a unique form of science, designed to explore and reveal unknown areas of growth. The growth thinking methodology brings this science into an actionable design method, whereby growth hackers can practice this science to identify unseen growth opportunities not yet being exploited, and turn them into growth capabilities and capacity.

With that out of the way, how do we tackle the big question:

"How do I hire a growth hacker?"

There are some aspects of this question that are not covered in this book; that is, 'What is a growth hacker?' but several other resources tackle this and may be accessed here: www.mygrowth-thinking.com/blog however, what we will be tackling is the:

1. Sharpest,
2. Boldest,
3. Most creative, and
4. Least known hacks for hiring growth hackers.

The hacks presented are designed to stimulate your own recruitment process within the context of your process and industry. Some of the hacks may not be applicable for many reasons; on the other hand, several of them can be combined to create new hacks in the context of your own situation.

This book will systematically guide you toward identifying individual hacks that you can execute, giving you the ability to combine hacks to create your own *and an understanding of how to detect if your competition is applying these hacks to you.*

The gloves are off, as this book will level the playing field when it comes to hacks being used by very few, giving them a competitive advantage.

Why this book is important

With the shortage and difficulty in gaining access to growth hackers and experts in the growth space, recruitment is a serious challenge. This is not something new; many industries have experienced this exact phenomenon. What is important are fresh, dynamic and effective ideas that can be used to recruit the best talent, quickly, effectively and with impact.

The demand for growth experts is growing, but with a fragmented and emerging discipline on the rise, and an ailing economic situation in the backdrop, the pressure is on. Talent is the key to making growth work, and in today's world with exponential technologies, the skills and methods that need to be employed for growth are becoming even more challenging to develop.

Your competitors are ***already employing these dirty secrets***, and most companies have no idea what is happening right in front of them. This books offers two very important strategies:

1. Advancing your recruitment strategy to capture the best talent
2. Decoding your competitors' moves on your own talent

This book is about understanding how to tackle these two issues and helping you to solve them.

Who this book is for

This book is for all of those who are involved in the recruitment process, both directly and indirectly. Direct involvement includes:

1. People and culture
2. Talent acquisition
3. Talent acquisition manager
4. Talent acquisition recruiter
5. Talent acquisition specialist
6. Talent acquisition recruitment
7. Talent manager
8. Talent partner
9. Talent management
10. Human resources recruitment
11. Human resources recruiter
12. Human resources consultants
13. Recruitment
14. Recruitment consultants
15. Recruiters
16. Executive search
17. Executive search recruiter
18. Executive recruiter
19. Executive search manager

Indirect involvement refers to those who are principal business owners or the person responsible for the recruitment request itself.

1. CEO - Chief Executive Officer
2. CTO - Chief Technology Officer
3. CMO - Chief Marketing Officer
4. CFO - Chief Financial Officer
5. Director
6. President
7. Founder
8. Executive director
9. Vice president
10. Manager

Anyone involved in the recruitment process will benefit from this book. This helps recruiters double down on an ever-challenging space. This book tackles four levels of decision-makers. First are executives who are leading growth; second are marketing function experts; third are growth function experts; and finally, recruitment and talent function experts.

How to use this book

This book has two broad objectives. The first is to help with actively recruiting top talent, and the second is to detect when your competition is hacking your talent. By understanding the dirty secrets exposed in this book, you will have gained *eight ways* of using the hacks:

1. **Single one-off** - use one hack, one time only
2. **Single continuous** - use one hack, continuously
3. **Multiple one-off** - use more than one hack, one time only
4. **Multiple continuous** - use more than one hack, continuously
5. **Combined one-off** - combine more than one hack, one time only
6. **Combined continuous** - combine more than one hack, continuously
7. **New hack one-off -** use existing hacks to generate a new one, one time only
8. **New hack continuous -** use existing hacks to generate a new one, continuously

These eight approaches give you a systematic approach to adopting all of the dirty hacks in this book for your own usage. The new hacks can be synthesized from the existing ones, whether as a combination, a one-off or multiple applications into a completely new recruitment hack not covered here. There are five aspects of how to use this book:

1. **Implement recruitment hack** - hire the best possible talent and retain them

2. **Performance of hacks** - test the performance of the recruitment hacks implemented
3. **Generate new hacks** - use existing recruitment hacks to generate for your own hiring
4. **Combined hacks** - Use high performing hacks and combine them to create new ones
5. **Detect growth hackers hacking you** - detect who is poaching your talent and counter them quickly and effectively.

These recruitment hacks are designed to amplify your chances of winning the war on growth talent globally.

How this book is structured

The book has three parts. The first part is about the bigger picture related to the war on talent in the growth hacking space. The second part covers the demand and the dynamics behind hiring growth hackers. The third part is 666+ growth hacks for hiring a growth hacker, broken down into 21 categories. The structure of the 666+ recruitment hacks is based on three levels of grouping:

1. **Category of hacks (21)** - broad set of recruitment hacks
2. **Group of hacks (84)** - more specific segments of hacks
3. **Hacks (668)** - specific recruitment hacks

At each level is an exclusive hack in itself, but the organizational hierarchy is designed to allow the reader to quickly navigate the hacks.

How you will benefit from this book

There are several ways in which you can benefit from this book. The biggest advantage is enabling yourself to tap into some of the industry's dirtiest secrets you didn't know about. Another big benefit is the ability to implement a structure and flow of ideas to help you directly within the context of your recruitment challenges.

1. Implement a **single** idea directly
2. **Combine** several ideas to form a new one
3. Support your existing recruitment process with a **new idea**
4. Generate new ideas **stimulated** from these ideas
5. **Detect** competition hacking your talent

A word of warning: some of these secrets are borderline ethically challenging. They may not suit your organization's guidelines and hence we advise you to take those hacks and adjust them to suit your internal governance. These ideas are destined to save you time and money and, most importantly, identify areas you have not yet seen or experienced.

Introduction

The science of exponential growth is quickly developing and, with the macroeconomic challenges surfacing, the demand on exponential growth has never been so great. With the talent shortage, limited data, limited methodologies, newly emerging tools, and a widely fragmented community, the growth space is potent with opportunity.

By 2030, 1 million growth hackers will be needed to satisfy the current need for experts in the sciences of exponential growth. The gap between skilled, qualified talent and growth requirements continues to widen. The pace and depth of this is alarming as startups, unicorns and even Fortune 500s struggle to retain and grow their growth talent.

Growth hackers talent gap
Supply Vs. Demand on growth hacking talent

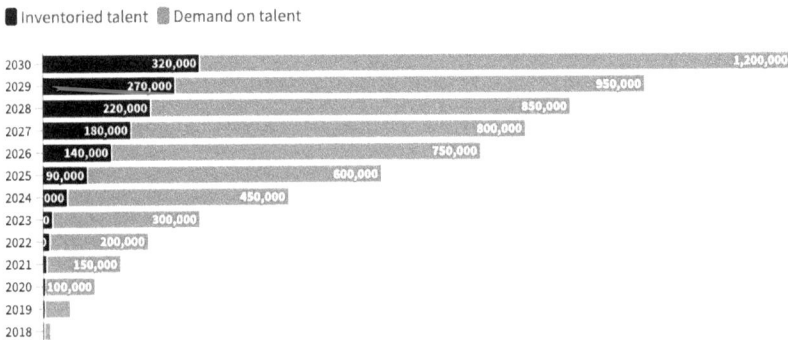

■ Inventoried talent ▨ Demand on talent

Year	Inventoried talent	Demand on talent
2030	320,000	1,200,000
2029	270,000	950,000
2028	220,000	850,000
2027	180,000	800,000
2026	140,000	750,000
2025	90,000	600,000
2024	000	450,000
2023	0	300,000
2022		200,000
2021		150,000
2020	100,000	
2019		
2018		

Growth will be challenged due to several factors in the growth hacking space. First is the relevance of existing education. This includes the coverage of topics, techniques and qualifications of the execution of skills. It also includes keeping abreast of rapid changes and shifting dynamics.

Second is the availability of talent that can execute the needed skills. Although many may present variables with existing skills, the issue is the rapid on-the-job skills development. Many organizations are not ready for this, let alone aligned with their strategy and able to be agile with shifting dynamics.

Third is the cross-functional skill change, whereby growth hackers need multiple skillsets. Most skills are packed into marketing and digital marketing-oriented skill sets, which aren't sufficient for hacking growth.

The economy is predicted to continue to shift in the coming years, potentially to the end of the decade, making it the longest running recessionary period we have seen yet. With that in the backdrop, as well as the acceleration of technology, pressure on skill adoption and the net outcome of growth, very challenging problems are presented to organizations of all sizes, industries and geographies.

Global Real GDP Growth Rates
Real GDP Growth Rates (Average Annual Percent Change)

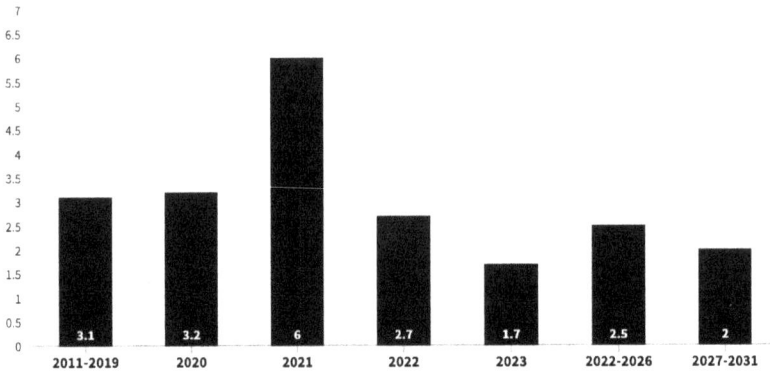

	2011-2019	2020	2021	2022	2023	2022-2026	2027-2031
	3.1	3.2	6	2.7	1.7	2.5	2

Source: The Conference Board Global Economic Outlook (September 2022) · NOTE
Global and EM annual GDP aggregation is based on China alternative. See Harry Wu, China's Growth and Productivity Performance Debate Revisited—Accounting for China's Sources of Growth with a New Data Set, The Conference Board, 2014. The data was updated and revised in September 2021 and the historical data series are available through The Conference Board Total Economy Database, United States (Adjusted) refers to our alternative GDP series, which are revised upward as they are based on alternative price deflators for ICT investment goods and services. Indian fiscal year begins in April, so the reported fiscal year growth rate refers to Q2-Q4 of year t and Q1 of year t+1 of the calendar year. Regions are aggregated based on nominal GDP in international dollars (PPP converted).

In response to a shrinking economy, demand for skills, and new emerging tools, the science of exponential growth is at center stage. In this book we will tackle one of the most vital components of success, which is talent. Despite the availability of new methods, tools, and technologies, the lowest common denominator will always be talent.

In this book, we will tackle and expose some of the dirtiest hacks used in their most raw form to help talent acquisition experts and heads of growth to lead their teams and organizations into the next battleground of the war on growth talent.

THE BIG question is "How do I hire a growth hacker?" and this is what we will tackle.

HIRE ME IF YOU CAN

Part 1
The Talent explosion

What is growth, a growth hacker, and the purpose of growth in an organization?

There are some basics that need to be defined and understood before moving forward. As an emerging discipline, it's important to understand definitive concepts in the field. Often, the next question after "how do I hire a growth hacker" is one of the following:

1. What is a growth hacker?
2. What does a *growth hacker* do?
3. What does a *growth unit* look like?

The three primary questions align hiring, talent, and placement. For growth to work, talent must be superseded by a strategy that dictates a structure to support it, and then talent to make the strategy happen via the organizational structure. This is why the three align in terms of how to hire, which talent to place, and where to place them.

This assessment will give you a quick and simple way to understand growth talent in a functional order, broken down into four major categories.

Growth talent assessment and alignment			Strategy	Structure	Talent
Assessment to align key components for growth to work			Yes, No	Yes, No	Yes, No
Function	1	Not a financial function			
	2	Growth is a stand-alone function			
	3	Strategic functional level with top functional priority			
	4	Growth function is to generate, sustain, and expand revenue			
Focus	5	Focus on Top line revenue growth			
	6	Optimization of Bottom line revenue growth			
	7	Integration of Hybrid revenue growth			
	8	Cross-functional incorporation of growth activities			
Apply	9	Use/create advanced methodologies for revenue expansion			
	10	Use/create advanced technology for revenue expansion			
	11	Run, develop and deploy rapid experimentations			
	12	Use technology and methodologies to scale and automate			
Develop	13	Develop, deploy, and sustain full-scale operations			
	14	Rapid and practical learning and training systems			
	15	Adopt to rapid changes quickly, harness new developments			
	16	Create new markets, products, and applications not used before			

The first category in the hierarchical order is function focus, application and development. Each one represents the definition of a growth hacker based on top-level job functions. Function is based on the purpose of the role; focus is the strategic functionality of growth; application is putting the strategies into action; and development is closing the loop by taking the full cycle to the next level.

Function - purpose of growth

1. **Not a financial function -** the role of a growth hacker is not to take responsibility for a financial function by supporting it.
2. **Growth is a stand-alone function** - The growth function itself is not to be nested structurally under another function but rather to stand alone
3. **Strategic functional level with top functional priority** - growth is a strategic function and to operate as a top priority function.
4. **Growth function is to generate, sustain and expand revenue** - the main functional goal of growth is to acquire, sustain and grow gross revenue.

Focus - strategic direction and priorities

5. **Focus on Top line revenue growth** – identifying, securing and growing gross revenue opportunities that do not exist.
6. **Optimization of Bottom line revenue growth** - optimizing and aligning existing resources to gain the highest utility possible
7. **Integration of Hybrid revenue growth** - aligning both top and bottom line growth to work together as effectively as possible

8. **Cross-functional incorporation of growth activities** - growth is a priority that should sit higher than operational functions, bringing them together in a cross-functional format

Apply - execution of growth hacking

9. **Use/create advanced methodologies for revenue expansion** - find, develop or configure the optimal business methodologies that best suit your growth formula
10. **Use/create advanced technology for revenue expansion** - find, develop or configure the optimal advanced technology that best suits your growth formula
11. **Run, develop and deploy rapid experimentations** - operate a very well-structured and highly optimized experimentation practice for growth hacking
12. **Use technology and methodologies to scale and automate** - combine methods and technology to scale and automate growth hacks into operational functions

Develop - expand on growth hacking successes

13. **Develop, deploy, and sustain full-scale operations** - capability to take growth hacks and turn them into long-term sustainable operational functions
14. **Rapid and practical learning and training systems** - learning and development systems that connect past learning to future experiments
15. **Adopt to rapid changes quickly, harness new developments** - detect, understand and effectively use changes that provide significant growth opportunities

16. **Create new markets, products, and applications not used before** - develop new greenfield growth opportunities, aligning markets, products and offerings.

This is a definitive guide to answering the question of what a growth hacker is as well as what their function is in any organization. Also, the book will explain how to align strategy structure and talent for growth. It gives a *systematic and prioritized breakdown of function*, and its alignment to develop, support and sustain long-term growth.

Where organizations focus their efforts for growth is very important. When optimizing for exponential growth, different types of organizations take different approaches. Optimization has worked best, for example, where unicorns (a unicorn is a startup company valued at $1 billion or more) have built their foundations on exponential growth.

Optimizing organizations for growth

Focal areas by type of organizations optimizing for exponential growth based on where they place their most efforts

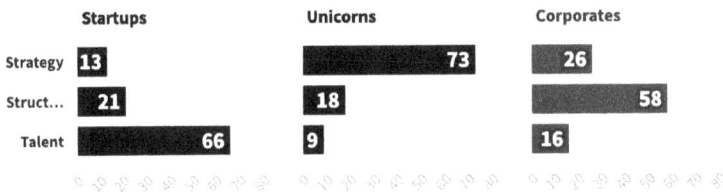

	Startups	Unicorns	Corporates
Strategy	13	73	26
Struct...	21	18	58
Talent	66	9	16

NOTE
This is a measure of where organizations focus there efforts on optimizing their organizations for exponential growth

When optimizing, there are three high level levers: strategy, structure and talent. When the three are aligned in priority order, they enable exponential growth to work. The priority order that works best for exponential growth is strategy, structure and talent. The reasons for this are:

1. Strategy creates clarity and direction
2. Structure enables that clarity and direction
3. Talent makes that clarity and direction happen with the right structures

This alignment isn't easy, but when optimized, it paves the way for major strides forward in developing exponential growth. The book Ready, Set, Growth Hack takes a deeper look at this alignment and explains how to build or rebuild organizations towards exponential growth.

ROI based on organizational optimization for growth

Return on investment based on organizational transformations that have growth as their goal by measuring the returns based on their optimization priorities.

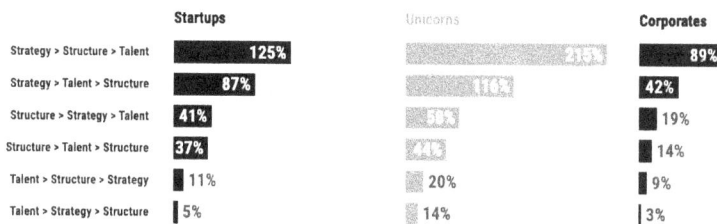

	Startups	Unicorns	Corporates
Strategy > Structure > Talent	125%	215%	89%
Strategy > Talent > Structure	87%	110%	42%
Structure > Strategy > Talent	41%	50%	19%
Structure > Talent > Structure	37%	24%	14%
Talent > Structure > Strategy	11%	20%	9%
Talent > Strategy > Structure	5%	14%	3%

Source: Hiring a growth hacker report - NUEL
This is a measure of returns on transformation programs designed to optimization organizations for growth based on organization type. The measures are based on organizations that have successful completed a transformation and have measured their returns.

Unicorns have had higher rates of success by far than startups and corporations. The leading optimization pattern is Strategy > Structure > Talent. When strategy sets clear direction, followed by a structure that supports it, then talent can perform.

Once the optimization patterns adjust, even with strategy leading, results drop to almost half. When talent supersedes structure, then a strategy will not be effectively executed. Growth companies have figured this out, and have conducted several transformational programs to adjust their organizational configurations.

The shortage of talent and tipping point of disruption

In 2019 it was estimated that there were roughly 5,000 growth hackers – a number hard to believe at that time, and now. This number was calculated based on those who are experts in the science of exponential growth, not digital marketers or other marketers labeling themselves as growth hackers.

This often led to misunderstandings around what is defined as the growth sciences and growth hacking. The field is an emergent discipline and its term was only coined in 2009-2010.
The coining wasn't the end point but rather the starting point, as previous practices of growth sciences had not been documented or defined as growth but were rather studied under the guise of other disciplines.

The coining of the term growth hacking marked the crossover point of bringing a fragment practice of growth sciences to a meeting point between several sub-disciplines and a defined practice. However, we are in a much different situation now and heading to a major talent crisis and a disruptive tipping point.

The shortage of talent and tipping point of disruption

Comparison of total headcount of talent needed vs. estimated revenue growth and economic growth as a percentage of **forecasted growth by year**

■ Talent gap ■ Est. Economic Growth ▓ Est. Increase In Revenue

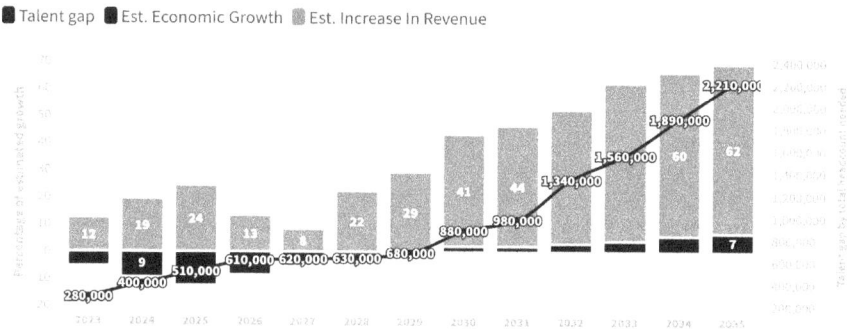

NOTE
This measures the estimated and forecasted economic growth rate vs. estimated expected revenue targets against the talent short, which is demand minus supply leaving the talent available

In 2029, a massive tipping point is expected, where the market will be missing roughly 680,000 growth hackers, with an expected flat economic growth outlook, and an expected average of 29% increase in revenue. This tipping point incorporates a few fundamental shifts that will take place:

1. A shift from flat, to slight increase in economic growth, which will be a dramatic transformation from flat, to the start of an uprising growth rate
2. Consistent pressure on firms to drive revenue up will no longer contrast the comic tend but will start to align with economic growth

3. The contrast in economic and revenue growth will magnify the shortage in growth hacking talent in 2029-2030
4. Talent development is underway today, but will hit a conclusion course of training, development and placement misalignment when the 2029-2030 tipping point kicks in
5. Continued pressure on revenue will become unrealistic for most firms, based on their inability to attract, retain talent and align that within their internal growth capabilities
6. Although 2030 sounds far away, it's not and it's fast approaching. Taking immediate, bold actions is crucial for growth success

The best-equipped organizations existing today are unicorns. 97% of unicorns use growth hacking as their main strategy, which has been what defines unicorns. These are startup companies with $1 billion or more. From the day they have been defined and traced, it is estimated that 1,500-2,000 unicorns exist today, with 50% of them in the United States alone.

At the center of the practice is a discipline, which is the tipping point of disruption. When done right, you scale at a massive speed, but if not done right, you die.

Once this tipping point is crossed, a more definitive market structure will form the organization growth market into much more effective segments. The nature of new practices is that they have several bleeding points where overlap creates confusion, which is where we are now, but by 2029 this will change.

A quickly emerging yet fragmented discipline

Growth hacking is a quickly growing discipline and more methods and structure are being applied to the practice. The nature of the growth hacking world is highly fragmented. Part of this issue is clusters of growth hackers who mostly come from a similar background and consolidate their own thinking.

Although this might sound like a positive thing, it distorts and disconnects a wider form of perspective. The wider the perspective, and the better the methods of capturing those wider perspectives, the more successful growth hacking will be.

Growth hacking skillset fragmented

Impact of skillset fragmentation based on return on investment and the widening gap of a talent shortage

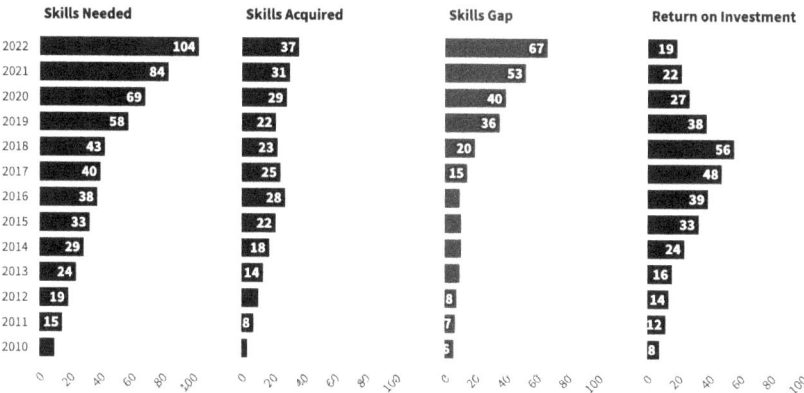

Year	Skills Needed	Skills Acquired	Skills Gap	Return on Investment
2022	104	37	67	19
2021	84	31	53	22
2020	69	29	40	27
2019	58	22	36	38
2018	43	23	20	56
2017	40	25	15	48
2016	38	28		39
2015	33	22		33
2014	29	18		24
2013	24	14		16
2012	19		8	14
2011	15	8	7	12
2010			5	8

NOTE
Skills are based on the number of skills counted ased in needed, and actually acquired, against an average Return on investment within the same period of measure of skills for growth.

Fragmentations will continue for years to come. As the talent gap widens, return on investments will decline. There are a few factors causing this, including the misalignment of talent, poor acquisition of talent, misalignment of goals and talent-poor structure without any strategy to support talent, as well as not keeping up with the skills needed.

Rapidly changing hiring needs will be your biggest priority

Recruiting isn't just more important today—it's also more difficult. That's because companies' talent needs seem to change day by day

Keeping up with rapidly changing hiring needs	65
eping up with recruiting technology	52
eraging data effectively	43
howing business impact	43
encing business leaders	41

Source: LinkedIn - The Future of Recruiting

Recruitment will continue to be a challenge, but even more so in a post-pandemic environment. With a massive shift in the use of automation, artificial intelligence and data analytics, the game has changed. Not also for hiring, but for the business functions from within.

The glue that holds this all together is growth. Hiring the best growth talent is going to be essential to this equation working. Recruiting the right growth expert isn't easy right now and will only get more difficult in the next 5-7 years.

What growth talent wants

Growth experts have different demands, ideas, expectations and perspectives on the future. Treating them like any other recruits will not work. They place more importance on things like learning, new technologies and methods and a wider range of freedom on experimentation.

What growth talent really wants

Priorities, and level of importance for a growth expert to successfully do their job and be happy. These are factors that motivate and stimulate.

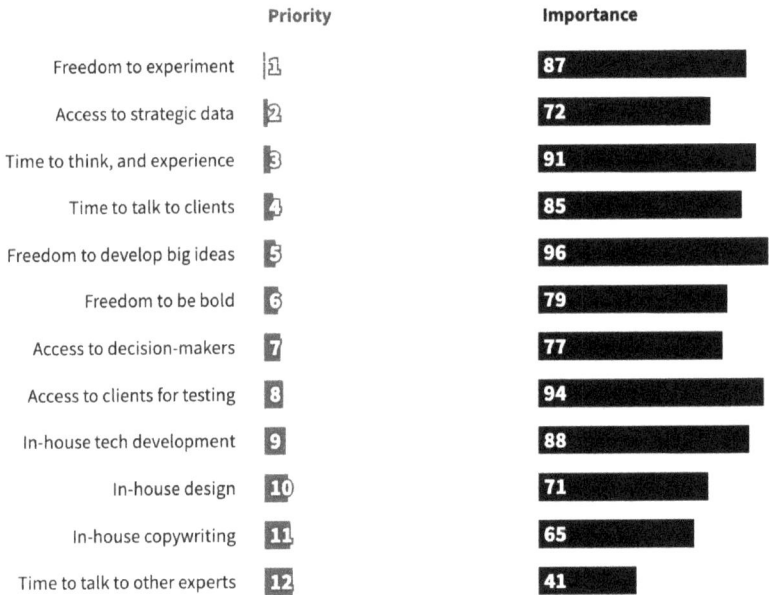

	Priority	Importance
Freedom to experiment	1	87
Access to strategic data	2	72
Time to think, and experience	3	91
Time to talk to clients	4	85
Freedom to develop big ideas	5	96
Freedom to be bold	6	79
Access to decision-makers	7	77
Access to clients for testing	8	94
In-house tech development	9	88
In-house design	10	71
In-house copywriting	11	65
Time to talk to other experts	12	41

NOTE
This is an assessment of growth experts to understand what motivates them to be attracted to a job role or to continue working in an existing job role

The focal areas for motivation and stimulation are the freedom to create, in-house resources, strategic access and time to perform.

Freedom to create is the leading element by giving growth hackers the space to experiment and create new growth hacks.

This is followed by in-house resources, allowing employees to quickly implement and learn from experiments. Next is access to strategic data and decision-makers, to shorten the time and energy needed in getting executive decisions made for full-scale operations.

The final priority is the time and space to be themselves to absorb inputs and insights, reflect and, crucially, act on them. In priority, the order of focus areas is:

1. Freedom to create
2. In-house resources
3. Strategic access
4. Time to perform.

Freedom to create starts with the empowerment of employees to experiment and the willingness to take risks. Incentivize risk taking and the systems needed to capture learning in a rapid and flexible manner. This is then followed by the ability to develop much larger and broader ideas based on the success of smaller experiments. This includes the power to create new products and markets as well as pursuing new customer segments. Finally is the ability to be bold and unique, by taking significant but calculated risks.

In-house resources cut time, cost and effort in the freedom to create processes. Having an in-house technology team that can execute quickly and easily is vital. This is followed by a design team that can do the research, develop the consumer experiences, and then move towards the final product quickly. Finally, it is essential to have a copywriting team that can create persuasion in the product content, and marketing to support the product/service deployment.

Access to strategic resources such as top-level data is necessary to see the whole picture, but also to be as foresighted as possible. This is also important for strategic alignment for optimal execution. Second is access to decision-makers in order to remove silos in providing feedback, getting information and directions, but most importantly is buy-in. Finally, it is vital to have access to live clients to run product testing and get real feedback while scaling.

Time to think, and reflect on experiences, is a very important learning process as well as a vital professional development opportunity. A 360° aspect needs to be taken on this, firstly from a **personal perspective for personal time and space**, but also from a professional viewpoint to **explore potential**. Time and space are also needed to speak with clients without having to sell them anything. This is about focusing on the client's perspective and empathizing with their problems. Finally, it is important to provide access to outside experts who can shed light on new perspectives and future developments to be considered and implemented.

HIRE ME IF YOU CAN

Part 2
Growth hackers in demand

The outlier effect

A global venture capital fund in the UK, which had achieved $13 billion in investments over its lifetime, became stagnant in growth. When stepping back and taking a closer look at their performance, decisions, and the rationale used for their investment decisions, analyzing their performance by looking into their return on investment, they examined:

1. Companies they had invested in;
2. Companies for which they had performed due diligence but had not invested in; and
3. Companies they were interested in but had not performed due diligence or invested in.

The companies they had invested in yielded a 6x return over the lifetime of the fund, whereas those for which they had performed due diligence on but did not invest in got a 17x return. Even more interesting, the companies they had an interest in but had not done due diligence or invested in yielded a 56x return. The outcome was that the 56x was essentially composed of outliers, of which, they were:

1. Initially able to identify;
2. Able to analyze and understand; but
3. Not able to see the full growth opportunity in.

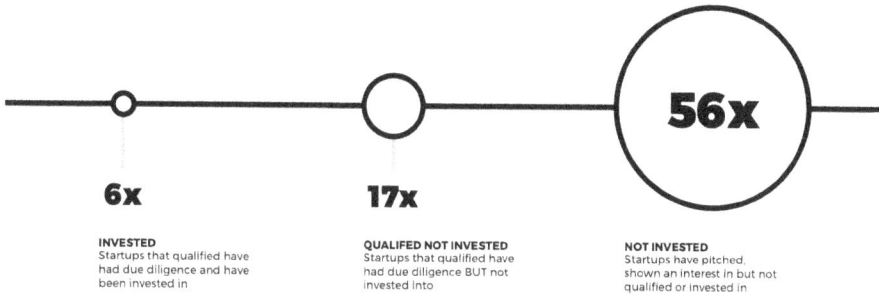

6x

17x

56x

INVESTED
Startups that qualified have
had due diligence and have
been invested in

QUALIFED NOT INVESTED
Startups that qualified have
had due diligence BUT not
invested into

NOT INVESTED
Startups have pitched.
shown an interest in but not
qualified or invested in

This fundamental understanding clearly identifies the problem of finding, investing in and ***growing outlier startups***. Although many venture capitalists pride themselves on this ability, in reality most cannot figure it out. The key components they evaluate do not measure up to a final result where an outlier would pass even their most basic screening criteria. This is something that applies across many funds, and in this particular case, this fund identified this problem and wanted to resolve it.

Furthermore, it was also identified through data that the baseline factors of idea, team, model, product-market fit, and funds in place were not relevant. Surprisingly, this can lead to the confusion of most fund managers as, without the basic building blocks, how can a company be investable at all?

Why outliers were missed

Comparison between reasons why outliers where declined vs attribution to success to measure how far off venture capitalists were off on their beats

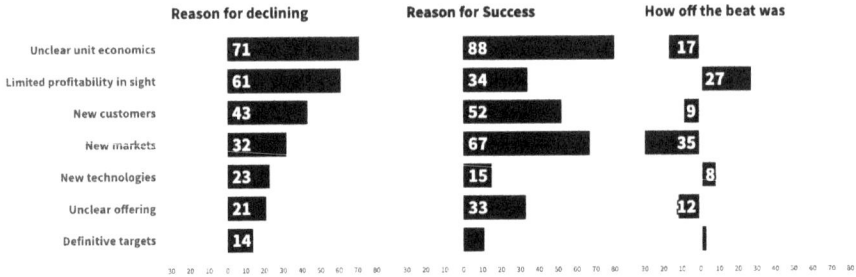

	Reason for declining	Reason for Success	How off the beat was
Unclear unit economics	71	88	17
Limited profitability in sight	61	34	27
New customers	43	52	9
New markets	32	67	35
New technologies	23	15	8
Unclear offering	21	33	12
Definitive targets	14		

NOTE

This assessment is based on a comparison of key factors why an investment would be declined or accepted. This is based on a weighted percentage given on how important that factor is. When comparing reason for declining and reason for success the difference is how on or off the beat was from initial judgment to final outcome

The number one cause of outliers being missed is forecasts of probability. A lack of insight into the existing market, as well as a very foggy foresight of profitability, is very challenging. This challenging predictability has the single most impact for missing the beat on outliers. Although it can be argued that the same case also exists with non-outlier investments, the predictability of profitability is still murky at best.

The second factor arises from tackling new technologies that are less predictable due to the vague nature of the technology itself. This doesn't apply to deep tech in all situations, but rather, in many cases, an advanced application of existing technology which then may throw off the prediction. This is then followed by a lack of definitive targets, which is natural when not all data points are known initially. This simply comes down to a matter of accepting, believing and managing ambiguity.

Next is tackling new customer behaviors and consumption patterns. This is often missed, as part of the growth hacking process is re-shaping consumption patterns. This can be seen with success stories such as Uber or airBNB, where companies successfully shift consumer behavior towards their type of offerings. Many of these startups use their base business model and technology as they grow to branch out into support services that eventually become spinoffs driving new revenue streams.

WHY OUTLIERS WERE MISSED - RANK ORDER

Limited profitability insight	1
Tackling new technologies	2
Lack of definitive targets	3
Tackling new customer behaviors	4
Unclear offering	5
Unclear unit economics	6
Tackling a new market	7

Roughly 70% of all venture capitalists admit to off-beats and those who are best at this celebrate it. They focus on how to continuously improve their process of finding and placing the best possible investments across disruptive landscapes.

Although many factors play into the investment decision, the factor that outweighs them all is growth. Even if you have a great product, that may not be enough; a good team can also be limiting, or an amazing model may also be insufficient. It is growth that makes all those other factors work, and the factor that makes investment worthwhile.

80% of venture capital firms in a **round A** (an investment in start-ups after showing progress, demonstrating the potential to grow and generate revenue) will demand that a startup has at least one head of growth. Some of the larger venture capital firms have their own growth teams internally, who support their collective portfolio.

1 million growth hackers by 2030

It is estimated that 1 million growth hackers are needed by 2030. This is a far cry from the estimated 10,000+ growth hackers within the ecosystem existing today (as of 2022). This massive gap leads to the number one question being asked:

1. In the 10 day growth hacking challenge,
2. At the end of keynote talks
3. During training courses, and
4. In general question-and-answer sessions about growth hacking.

Why is that? It's simple: they don't have the internal expertise, nor the access to them externally, and whatever they have done or used in the past has not worked. This leads to the main question of:

"How do I hire a growth hacker?"

As simple as the question is, the answer is highly complicated and it starts with the fact that we have **10,000** of them today and within **7 year**s we will need **1 million** of them.

1 million growth hackers by 2030

Demand vs. the supply of actual talent in the growth hacking space over the next decade

■ Inventoried talent ▓ Demand on talent

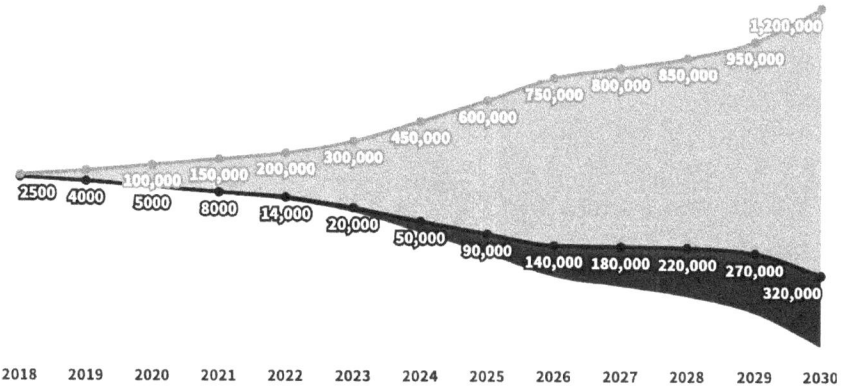

	2018	2019	2020	2021	2022	2023	2024	2025	2026	2027	2028	2029	2030
Demand	2500	4000	100,000	150,000	200,000	300,000	450,000	600,000	750,000	800,000	850,000	950,000	1,200,000
Inventoried	2500	4000	5000	8000	14,000	20,000	50,000	90,000	140,000	180,000	220,000	270,000	320,000

NOTE

These are estimates based on identifiable positions published and data collected based on positions in demand vs. the supply of talent actually available with the base skillset to execute growth hacking job functions

Although numbers may vary from different sources on this, you will find that the gap is still massive, and that is the issue with hiring a growth hacker.

Why is it hard to hire growth hackers?

It's a **new practice** that is in the process of structuring itself. Growth as a science is not offered in educational institutes, and dedication is fragmented across informal organizations. The informal organizations mostly focus on marketing and digital marketing skills, which is not growth.

The challenge is that growth is a cross-functional practice and requires many different skill sets. Hiring based on specific skillsets limits the growth hacking process and hence will always leave a gap. To master this, growth hackers need to focus on the growth hacking process itself, which is where all of the required functions are connected.

The main goal of the growth hacking process is to draw on the functions that are directly impacted, and manage the indirect ones that may be less visible in terms of implications and consequences. For example, if a growth hacker is highly marketing oriented, but has an operational consequence, this would lead to failure. However, taking the operational implications into account for the growth hack itself would then ensure a much higher success rate.

Why its hard to hire growth hackers

Skill acquisition vs. what is needed and actual application of skills are
widen fragmented impacting growth results

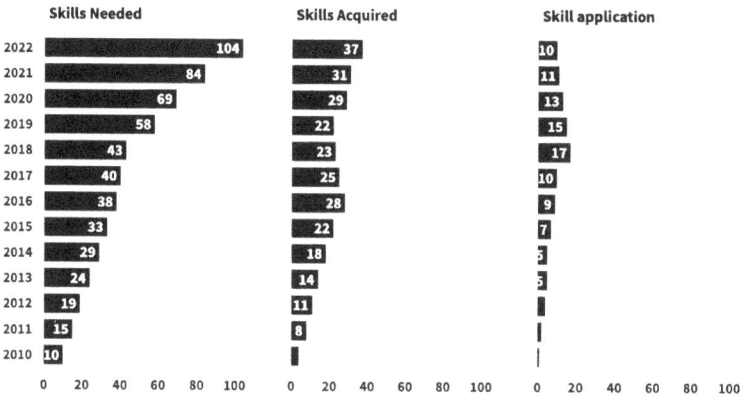

	Skills Needed	Skills Acquired	Skill application
2022	104	37	10
2021	84	31	11
2020	69	29	13
2019	58	22	15
2018	43	23	17
2017	40	25	10
2016	38	28	9
2015	33	22	7
2014	29	18	5
2013	24	14	5
2012	19	11	
2011	15	8	
2010	10		

NOTE
The penetration of skills being applied against time, effort and money invested in application of skill have a wide gap, and declining with time

The key issue is the rate of application of skills vs. the skills needed
and acquired. The wider this gap is, the more challenging the application of growth hacking skills becomes. The gap between needed
and acquired skills needs to be bridged first before the skill application improves. Although the application of skill may be what is seen
here, it's about the *lack of standardization* and agreed upon protocols in the growth industry itself that is the real issue.

Once standardized skilling is put into place on the industry side, the
needed and acquired skills gap will improve. This provides a focal
point where the best talent, based on the applicability of skill set,
will become much more viable. This visibility through standard mea-

sures in training and development will have a direct impact on the return of investment in skills and overall results.

Growth hacker hiring funnel

A hiring funnel is a sequence of steps taken to generate leads to hiring and all the way to on-boarding successful candidates. A hiring funnel is no different from a marketing or sales funnel; the aim is to find and recruit candidates.

Hiring Funnel for Growth Hackers

Hiring funnel, conversion rate, and efforts placed on each phase to improve the effectiveness of each step in the funnel

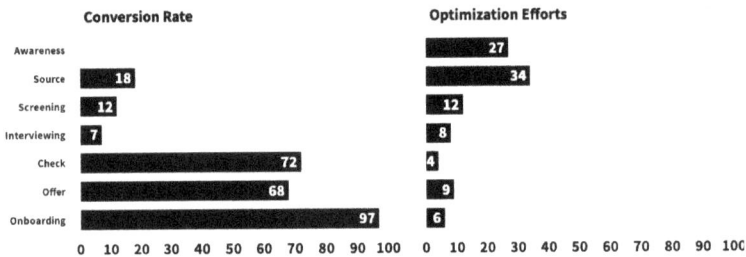

	Conversion Rate	Optimization Efforts
Awareness		27
Source	18	34
Screening	12	12
Interviewing	7	8
Check	72	4
Offer	68	9
Onboarding	97	6

NOTE
This is a measure of conversion which is success rate divided by total number from each step in the funnel. The efforts per step are measured by the amount of time, money and energy exerted to improve each step.

The hiring funnel for growth hackers, as with others, involves a basic 7 step process. The difference in our measures is specific to hiring candidates for growth positions. The following is a breakdown of the funnel steps:

1. **Awareness** - Create visibility for employment opportunities
2. **Source** - Generate leads which are potential candidates
3. **Screening** - Filter potential candidates
4. **Interviewing** - Qualify potential candidates for a fit
5. **Check** - due diligence on qualified candidates
6. **Offer** - extend a job offer to potential candidates
7. **Onboarding** - accept offer, and induct them into your organization

At the awareness and sourcing stage, the objective is to accurately target growth hackers. In the screening and interview stage, the aim is to qualify the skills and fit of the potential candidate on the growth team. Check and offer involve taking qualified candidates, ensuring they are a safe and low risk hire, and extending a competitive offer. Finally is on-boarding, which is the most critical part of shifting a candidate from the hiring process to employee status.

HIRE ME IF YOU CAN

Part 3
666 dirty hacks to recruit growth hackers

1. Stealing talent

The old-school classic method of talent acquisition is outright steal-ing the talent. It's a smart way of going about it, as previous perfor-mance is a good indicator of future performance. However, this game has changed and can get very dirty.

2. Steal them without stealing them

Do not hire them right away. Introduce yourself as a recruiter, and state your interest in only keeping in touch for future opportunities (give them a business card tailored to recruitment). This is a seed-ing strategy, whereby you are only opening the doors. The secret here is keeping your company at the forefront of their mind without actually proposing recruitment until the time is right. Keeping 'top of mind' can be achieved by sharing industry information or simply grabbing a coffee together or just saying hello. Of course, at each engagement point, you want to be adding value.

3. Throw a case at them

Reach out to them, put a growth hacking case in front of them and ask them for their help. **Propositioning this is a non-binding, no-conflict and low-friction exercise**. This is to be conducted on a friendly basis, to pick their brain and get their help on the issue. To ensure this happens, offer to pay them for their time and ask for lim-ited inputs just to see on a surface level what they can do, before going deeper. The secret behind this is to build a rapport, pave the way for a direct hire, and promote your firm's openness and willing-ness to work with talent in many different ways and formats.

4. Hire them for a small task

Beyond picking their brain and perhaps paying a small sum for their time, outright hire them as a side hustle for a small task. Give them something meaningful for you to test them on, something with a clear outcome and impact, and a task they can build on. Design this to be a low-friction, no-risk, and no-conflict engagement. You may use a third party to facilitate this, depending on your judgment. The secret behind this is paving the way to test out talent, without it being a formal hiring process. This enables your organizations to evaluate, engage and build on these initial interactions. Since it's paid, this means there will be feedback, and you can see how they perform in a committed situation, rather than a hypothetical scenario.

5. Invite them to an open coffee day

Build rapport, install trust and pave the way forward for a direct recruitment. Conduct an open coffee day, which is a 30-60 min event (physical, virtual or hybrid) in which the top decision-makers join with key people from your growth team. This is an informal setting for everyone to break the ice and get to know each other, and most importantly for top leaders to hear what the talent has to say. The secret behind this, as a leader, is demonstrating your openness to listen to outside ideas, your growth team's willingness to absorb diverse talent, and a workplace atmosphere where *hierarchy is greatly reduced*. This attracts new talent, builds rapport and paves the way in an informal setting for stealing talent from other firms quickly, easily and at a low cost.

6. Invite them to an event

Hosting an event, sponsoring one, or even just participating in another event can bring the talent you want to hire. If it is a major event with a higher barrier to entry, this would be more ideal, as it will be seen that you are taking the risk of inviting them or taking them with you. Ensure this is a no-risk, no-conflict and informal gesture and is done in good faith without any strings attached. The secret behind this is building rapport, investing in talent before even approaching them and seeing them in action at an event.

7. LinkedIn baiting profiles request intro for a job

Post a formal job at your firm. Use a LinkedIn profile, designed for baiting (a fabricated profile that is associated with your target hiring profile), to apply for the job. Get one profile to connect with your company page where the job is posted, and a completely different profile to connect with the target candidate. Have the profile connected to your target request an introduction to the profile, follow your company and apply. In the introduction request, clearly state the intention of the introduction is to get networked into that job opportunity, so your chances of success are higher. The secret behind this is to get that profile to ask the target candidate for their advice on how to secure such a position. This gives an opportunity for them to build rapport, and give advice. By doing so, this cements the opportunity for job placements at your company. By seeding this opportunity to your target candidate, when the job posting you actually want them for appears, the one who received advice can repay the favor by suggesting they apply for that post. Do this in passing so it's casual and soft in nature, to stimulate the target candidate to make the decision of applying.

8. Make them superstars before hiring them

Issue a new industry report or white-paper or broker a position within one about to be published, write it up and get the name of the growth hacker in that content. Of course, you do this with approval and convent and some inputs from there. The point is to make them look good, for doing little to nothing. It is a practice often used in the medical industry between pharma companies and doctors.

9. Sponsor them to speak at an event

Highlight their talent, and put money behind them. Sponsor them to speak at a third-party event under your banner. This way, they can see that you're invested in the event and in them, even if they work for someone else. This needs to be positioned as a career development opportunity. The secret behind this is to build rapport, get to know them, thank them afterward for their input, and then springboard from there. Spring-boarding involves highlighting some specific points they have raised, and showing that you are interested in deepening those thoughts and insights and use that as the gateway to directly hire them.

10. Get them nominated in your own awards

Establish your own awards and ranking systems. Rank the target hire and give them an award. Have several categories and participants, as well, to multiply the efforts with this exercise. The point is to get them in your sights, let them know they are valued, and initiate a low-friction, informal conversation with them. The secret behind this can be an active or passive approach, depending on your strategy. An active approach would mean having a conversation right after, and proceeding into a direct recruitment process. The passive strategy would be to keep them feeling recognized but top-of-mind; to actively recruit them, alter your strategy or trigger them to approach your firm for an opportunity,

11. Invite them to your open coffee day as an expert

After establishing their value and importance, invite them exclusively as an expert on a very specific topic. The idea behind an open coffee day is to have your top leadership and growth team present. The secret behind this is to motivate the target candidates by making them aware that your top leaders are listening and interested. By doing this, they are positioned as experts internally and have the opportunity to tap into their approach and thinking. Then build a path to recruiting them, based on this event.

12. Invite them to do a guest blog post

Another strategy is to tap into them by inviting them to write a guest blog on a specific topic. This gives you the power to get them focused on how to solve a specific growth hacking problem. By doing this, you enable them to gain more expert power outside their current organization, without irritating your competitors. The secret behind this is to bring them into your organization by building on the article itself. For example, you could let them know that your growth team liked the article and wanted to know more about a specific point. This paves the way for an informal conversation and rapport building to softly attract them into your growth team without your competition detecting it.

13. Invite them on your own podcast as an expert

This works just like the guest blog strategy; do the same but in a podcast format. You can host your own or, if you have a relationship with an existing podcaster, bring them on as a placement. This will differ based on your strategy and resources. Again, the secret behind this is to build rapport, tap into their expertise, and then recruit them in a soft manner, without your competitors detecting the recruitment activity.

14. Fabricating a talent war

Get a competitor to hire your other competition's talent knowingly. It's an old dirty hack, whereby you turn your competitors against each other and force them to lock down their own talent (i.e. ensure their employees do not defect and move elsewhere). When they are locked down, the talent doesn't like this and gets edgy. Since two or more of your competitors are already wary of each other - but not you, since you have not entered this talent war - you're ready to hire. Your competitors will know they will lose their talent and will have to use hacks to keep them, but this is when you swoop in before this happens and before the talent is locked in. Your timing has to be on the mark.

15. LinkedIn recruiter baiting

Set up a third-party recruiter profile not linked to your organization at all. Have that baiting profile directly recruited from your target candidate's organization but not your direct target. Use this to expose sloppy handling and protocols in the communication process, exposing the client - that being another competitor. Distract your competitor with a target on another candidate. Meanwhile, take advantage of this distraction to directly pursue the target candidate.

The secret behind this is to induce apprehension in terms of another candidate you don't want to hire, and another competitor. This distraction allows you to move below the radar without suspicion and target the actual candidate with less friction.

16. Fabricated job board posting

Create a fabricated job board posting by a third party, that is representing a position that is identical to one already at your competitors, where you can plan to recruit from. Using 5-10 LinkedIn baiting profiles, share this post with people at that firm in different unrelated places, asking for a direct connection to whoever is responsible for that post being advertised. Remember, you can combine hacks to optimize. Ensure this doesn't target your target candidates, of course, but others close to them (other team members). The secret here is to create confusion. In the midst of this confusion, no one really knows what is happening and this forces the candidate to become more cautious, which means they are more alert. Tap into that heightened state of alertness and recruit them, showing there is demand on their team, and they cannot detect whether it's real or not.

17. Fabricate your competitors' presence for recruitment

This can get dicey at best. Use an email address that includes your competition's domain as a fabricated email. Position the outreach emails as a direct recruitment email to specific candidates you don't want to hire at that organization. This will create another form of confusion and a decoy that allows you to focus on actually recruiting the target candidate you want. The secret behind this is also related to creating decoys and confusion and positioning your competition against the target organization where you plan to hire. Although this can be done in many different ways, it is best to use good judgment in deciding what would best work for you.

18. Fabricate a downsizing

This will require some very careful coordination. When downsizing comes into play, employees become nervous and worry about their future. If an actual downsizing is happening at this particular time, this is the time to strike. If there is not an active downsizing taking place, all it takes are some very simple rumors to float among the right circles. This can be done in a few ways using direct means; for example, employees who work for you could pass on this type of information as though they've heard it from a third-party sauce. Another strategy is the placement of this type of information in forums, blogs or other forms of online community, where information is openly shared. The secret is to use this opportunity, when employees are apprehensive about the future of that organization, to directly recruit.

19. Covering the basics to start with

We have to start somewhere, so let's discuss the basics and examine how to find and hire the best growth hackers. If we nail down the basics first, this gives us a foundation to work with as we growth hack the hiring process.

20. Freelancer websites

This is an obvious start, so let's look at the best places to search and how to hack the search for a growth hacker. First, here is a list of the 16 top freelancer websites.

- Fiverr
- Toptal
- Jooble
- Freelancer.com
- Upwork
- Flexjobs
- SimplyHired
- Guru
- People Per Hour
- ServiceScape
- TaskRabbit

Now we have got that out of the way, what's the secret to finding the right growth hacker? Since they are focused on skills, rather than the practice of growth hacking, you have to search for skills. Many of them will list their skills based on the idea they are in demand and it's what non-experts will search for.

There are 200+ listed sub-skills used by growth hackers. Remember, not all of them are pure growth hackers, but rather digital marketers. A growth hacker is not a digital marketer. Use the following search skills to narrow down your search for a growth hacker.

1. Automation
2. Back-linking & Outreach

3. Business Strategy
4. Conversion Rate Optimization
5. Google Analytics
6. Growth Hacking
7. Lead Generation
8. Lead Nurturing
9. Marketing Automation
10. Public Relations
11. Search Engine Marketing
12. Search Engine Optimization
13. Social Media Content Creation
14. Social Media Optimization
15. Web Scraper
16. B2B Marketing
17. Data Science
18. Data Scraping
19. Email Marketing
20. Internet Research
21. Landing Page
22. List Building
23. Marketing Strategy
24. Off-page Optimization
25. Outreach Strategy
26. Paid Media
27. PPC Marketing
28. Python
29. SEO Audit
30. SEO Back-linking
31. SEO Keyword Research
32. Social Media Marketing

33. Customer Relationship Management
34. Email Campaign Setup
35. Inbound Marketing
36. Mozenda Scraper
37. SaaS
38. ScrapeBox
39. Scrapy
40. Shopify

21. Many small tasks, progressive simulation

The great thing about freelancers is that you can test them out before ever attempting to hire them. The key here is to set a series of small tasks. Each one should get progressively more difficult and each should be linked to each other. The set of tasks should be related to a real growth hacking problem you're currently solving. Ideally, you should have 5-10 tasks, all connected, and a pool of 10-12 freelancers per campaign you run. You will need to pay them and if they are not motivated when paid, they are disqualified immediately, or if they don't take paid work seriously, they are disqualified. The secret behind this is being able to test for speed, accuracy, qualification, creativity and finally the result itself. As you run the progressive tasks, the freelancers need to be put into three categories: those who qualify; those who don't qualify but might improve; and those who have done an average job but have the potential to improve. The reason we point towards getting a positive result is that the progressive tasks allow you to see their progression live. And this progression is the most important part of this hack.

22. Pre-engaged before tasking

The pre-engagement stage is vital for communication and ensuring a good outcome. This stage costs nothing and enables you to understand who you're working with. By asking key questions, for example, and asking for their opinions to see their thought processes, this will guide you towards those who will potentially perform well. Start with qualification questions, such as the following examples: Have you growth hacked BLANK before? If you have growth hacked BLANK before, what was the result and why? If you were to re-do this growth hacking BLANK, what would you do differently? Such qualification questions give you a progressive line of inquiry from top level to lower details without wasting much time. After this, ask more strategic questions, such as how did you go about this and why, and what steps were taken and what can be improved. Remember, in many ways, this is a light interview. After that, throw the high level scope of what you want, and then ask them how they would go about this. Have 3-5 questions prepared asking what they would do if something specific went wrong. This helps you to see their problem solving skills and their ability to anticipate problems in advance. The secret is to get a taste of what is to come as quickly as possible and pre-qualify. One final tip: it would be a wise idea not to use your brand on freelancer sites so they will treat you the same as any other organization coming through the doors.

23. Failed case, urgent help

Build a case; ideally, a realtime one you're tackling for growth. Articulate it in a brief, clear and concise manner, and tell them you need an urgent solution. Showing urgency and also desperation might work very well in this situation. Use your good judgment, of course. The key here is to show that they are needed now and that the problem needs to be solved quickly, but without hiring them, you need to know they are the right person for the job. This gives you a sense of how committed they are and how clear they want to be before making a commitment, but also gives an opportunity for pre-qualifying their thinking skills and approach. The secret behind this is **showing failure upfront**, giving them a sense of urgency and the space to problem-solve. The key here is to see how they problem-solve within a tight timeframe and limited scope. It would be wise to have a budget in place, but also to spend as much time and effort on the pre-qualification part before putting them on the case. Remember to provide technical details such as what has been tried, what technology has been used, and all the possible failure points that can be leveraged to solve the case.

24. Ask for a freelancer referral

Freelancers know freelancers, and this is where asking for a referral can become powerful. Most freelancers will know someone who can support their work, enhance their work or, more importantly, fill in the gap in their work. On freelancer sites, where more micro-tasks are taken on, this will be more viable; on the large task sites, it will be a case of asking for someone to work on the project. The key to this is networking. The secret is to tap into networks beyond utilizing your own existing experts.

25. Get them to recruit for you

Most freelancer platforms will have a customer success and support team, designed to help you find what you want. Why not outsource it to them, and let them do the work for you? There are two main outcomes here: the first is to learn from them how they get the best results, as they know their system best; the second is getting them to do the legwork for you. The secret behind this is tapping into their own experience on how best to navigate their own platform and get you the best results. You may be able to go beyond this and see if they can provide an ongoing recruitment service for you, as it might be worth paying for them to do the recruitment for you on an ongoing basis. Taking that even one step further, you can have a monitoring and alert approach, so that when new talent becomes available, you're able to tap into it quickly.

26. In the middle of nowhere

Although you might be tempted to cover only the top freelancing websites, you should go for niche, smaller ones that cover places the big guys don't. Smaller and more niche platforms may be willing to play ball more with different options and greater flexibility. The secret behind this is to find these options to exploit and utilize them towards your own sourcing process. Approach a few discussion topics such as sponsorship, getting on their mailing list, hosting an event with them or taking part in one they are organizing.

27. Job boards

Job boards operate in a similar manner to the freelance sites, but the difference is the intentions. On freelancer sites, workers may not be actively seeking a new job, but on a job site they obviously are. Here is a list of top job boards to look into:

- Indeed Job Search
- Glassdoor Jobs
- Google for Jobs
- Monster
- ZipRecruiter
- Simply Hired
- CareerBuilder
- Snag Jobs
- LinkUp

Just like on the freelancer websites, use the sub-skills listed above. The difference here is that you will find deeper talent who have expertise in the whole growth hacking process. You want to pay close attention to their previous performance, actual revenue generated and their role in the growth hacking process.

28. Posting magnification and traffic hacking

Once you have a post on any of the major job boards, the portal should be gaining traction for filling your posts. That alone should be enough, in theory, but magnifying it gives you more traction and a longer shelf-life outside the portal itself. Copy the post, and place it outside the portal in high visibility areas pointing towards the post itself on the board. The secret to this is being able to distribute the URL to the post. This can be done by using URL submission sites, FREE PR distribution sites, blog posts on your own platform, placement of links in forums, social media and, of course, on your own hiring website.

	Free Submission Site	Website URL
1	Free Web Submission	https://www.freewebsubmission.com/
2	Active Search Results	https://www.activesearchresults.com/addwebsite.php
3	Buildwebsite4U	http://www.buildwebsite4u.com/tools/submission.shtml
4	Entire Web	https://www.entireweb.com/free_submission/submit/
5	Exact Seek	http://www.exactseek.com/add.html
6	Gigablast	http://www.gigablast.com/addurl
7	Infotiger	https://infotiger.com/addurl
8	Scrubtheweb	http://www.scrubtheweb.com/addurl.html
9	Submit Express	http://www.submitexpress.com/free-tools/free-website-submission/
10	Web Squash	https://www.websquash.com/submit.php
11	Google Search Console	https://search.google.com/search-console
12	Bing Webmaster Tools	https://www.bing.com/webmasters
13	Yandex	https://passport.yandex.com/
14	Baidu	https://ziyuan.baidu.com/login/index?u=/site/siteadd
15	Google News	https://publishercenter.google.com/

SOURCE: https://seochatter.com/free-web-submission-sites-search-engine/

Additional resources are Active Search Results, Buildwebsite4U, Entireweb, Exact Seek, Gigablast, Infotiger, Scrubtheweb, Submit Express, and Web Squash.

29. Release the job post into the wild

A lot like the free URL submission hack, this works in getting direct public relations exposure. There is a further strategic option of using high-end paid platforms, but the free ones serve the purpose in this hack. Free press releases essentially take your news and distribute it to the media and other media-related assets on the web. The releases are monitored by media to identify stories to cover, or to give more cover if the story is worth it. There are two ways of going about this: going fry and just announcing for SEO purposes; or really getting creative about your job opening and creating a story that would be worth picking up. Creating a story means getting very creative; it can include stories about people in your company, or a fabricated story about a superhero in that post, or it can be about facts and figures that are very interesting but well told, to gain interest. The creative options are endless but this may be the best way to make this hack work. The secret behind this is twofold; the first is the exposure and awareness element, and the second is the storytelling part. If you nail the storytelling part, this can get picked up by many other media outlets and blogs that will do the exposure work for you and drive more traffic to your post.

30. Job board asset raid

For each job board you are actively (or even inactively) posting on, find indirect assets such as blog posts, podcasts, slideshows, events, training etc and plug in. Multiply your efforts. Ideally, you will need to have an active job post on their platform to leverage your support and accelerate your exposure. In some cases, with careful navigation, you may be able to get away without having a post on their platform. This would be using the unique branding angels towards job weeks in the growth hacking space. The secret behind this is leveraging the native assets available on the job boards themselves and using them to amplify your presence, and the job posting itself. Engage on a series of placements rather than just on a one-off. This means investing heavily in good quality content and it's worth it in the long term.

31. Merch it, hack it

To traffic hack and increase exposure and volume towards your job board postings, create merchandise around the specific job posting. This taps into ecommerce traffic, and gives you a very hype and creative way to brand your growth hacking employment opportunities. When branding them, ensure they are hype, catchy, stand-out and desirable to buy. Use the specific position and even the job board branding if you can (within legal means - please use good judgment). The secret behind this is to tap into ecommerce traffic, and search engines optimize your job posting on the job board itself. There may need to be a judgment call in terms of whether you strategically place the post on your own website and do this, or in combination with the job board. The strategy is to create mass exposure to widen your net.

32. Urgency at its best

Use urgency at its best. Do this by posting growth hacking job openings, aside from your long-term consistent ones, that must be filled within 72 hours. (You can create extensions, but short ones, so it's not over-long.) Find options within the job board for this and utilize their systems and resources. It would be best to talk to them directly first and explain that it is urgent. Ask them what they can do for you. Let them guide you in terms of how to hack their system. The secret behind this is two main outcomes; either you fill the position, or you don't. The hack behind this is that if you don't fill it, you go back to the job board and complain in order to get further assistance to drive more effort into the post. If it is fulfilled, then job done. Utilize the job board support systems to enable your posting to become more effective quickly. Carry those lessons forward with your other postings, but the key is using the power of urgency.

33. Chatbot to job board

Create your own Chatbot on your hiring site and channel traffic to your job board posting. Although you may not want to channel traffic elsewhere, this makes your posting more popular on the job board and you leverage its greater reach. The secret behind this is leveraging and tapping into wider networks.

34. Google searches

The power of Google is undeniable, but how can you best use it wisely? Here are some search queries to use to find growth hackers.

1. "Growth hacker" + "Location"
2. "Growth hacker" + "Sub Skill"
3. "Growth hacker" + "Past clients"
4. "Growth hacker" + "Past projects"
5. "Growth hacker" + "Portfolio"
6. "Growth hacker" + "blog posts"
7. "Growth hacker" + "personal website"
8. "Growth hacker" + "expert" or "expertise"
9. "Growth hacker" + "Training" or "Trainer"
10. "Growth hacker" + "Coach" or "coaching"
11. "Growth hacker" + "Mentor" or "mentors"
12. "Growth" + "Mentor" or "Mentors

A combination of some of these queries will also generate some growth hackers. Remember that there are not really many of them out there. The idea is to take one step back and reverse the search to find them a bit deeper down.

35. Google alerts to capture talent

Use Google alerts to monitor layoffs and use that as a trigger to tap into talent that has become available and is actively searching for a job. This can be done in three formats. One is layoffs by second, layoffs by company and lastly, layoffs by geography. The alerts would need to be a string such as "company layoffs" or "company layoffs in Fashion" or "company layoff in Silicon Valley". The point is to create several well targeted alerts. Once you have chosen those alerts, head over to LinkedIn and start looking for employees in those firms. Many will already have tagged themselves as being open to jobs, and you can reach out to others who haven't. The secret here is that once you have identified these opportunities, you need to directly find growth hackers, or people with the same or similar skill sets who are looking to their next career development move. The ones who are seeking their next opportunity and want to transfer and transform their skills into the growth hacking field are the most potent of those in this pool. The key here would be having a great onboarding campaign to help bridge this gap to attract more and better candidates.

36. Google Jobs hacked

Go to https://jobs.google.com/ and directly post jobs. Although they have an aggregator tool to capture jobs via schema mark-up and other data collection methods, don't depend on that. Post directly into the Google Jobs site. Although this is covering some of the basics, how to hack this is simple. Focus on keeping posts open all the time, not just at times when you have active open roles. Post a wide variety of growth hacking roles, from entry point to senior, but do not miss out on posting growth hacking intern and apprentice jobs. The secret behind this is having several ongoing posts all the time, but the kicker is combining other native Google search optimization features such as Google images, docs, sheets, forms, podcast, and shopping.

37. Google images for recruitment hacked

Google gives priority to its own products to be the most searchable and discoverable. It all starts with you giving them permission to make it public, giving it a reference from your own website with proper link building structures. Take your job posting, and first turn it into an image. Turn it into a few images and optimize them towards your job opening on Google. For example, one image can be the job role itself, another can be an infographic about the job function and another can be testimonials of previous employees in the role. The point is that you want several images which you will title with the job role name and optimize towards the job opening. The secret behind this is using Google's native optimization for images towards your Google job opening. You can go further and post the images on Pinterest and other image search engines to spread the optimization capabilities. Repeat this for every role, reuse the images as templates but keep them as fresh as possible every single time.

38. Google docs, sheets, forms for recruitment hacked

A lot like the concept with Google images, you will take your job-related content and repurpose it into docs, sheets and forms. The doc can be the job role, and other technical content related to the job with a call to action and a direct link to the Google job posting itself. Be sure to make this Google doc public and searchable. To refinance its optimization, post links to the Google doc itself, as well as forms, comments, and other public places to show interest in the document. Don't forget to use your own website as well, if applicable. Repeat this process with a Google sheet, which can be a checklist with more content, and a Google form that can be a pre-qualification form. The concept is to get them all to link to the Google job posting. The secret behind this is popularizing each single job posting using native Google optimization priority. You can take this one step further and submit the links separately and to several submission directors; that also helps to push the backlinks to the documents themselves.

39. Google podcast for recruitment hacked

Just like the previous hacks, this strategy is to tap into native Google functions to optimize job visibility for recruitment. In this case, create a job-specific podcast with your brand on Google podcasts. Create a few episodes to the jobs you're hiring and title them towards those postings. Optimize the content in the episodes as well as towards the job post itself. Create an episode structure so the head of growth can be in the first episode talking about the growth team, growth challenges and some of the cool things they are doing. In the second episode, use this opportunity to build on the first and discuss the job role; conduct a mock interview, and interview people in the same role in other places or in the past to give some further depth to the job role. In the third episode, docs on job interview tips and tricks to prompt applicants to use them to apply for the job itself. The secret behind this is to always have a call to action in the episode itself and in the content as a link to the job opening itself. Guide them via the episodes to create interest, show you're open to bringing them on, and to making your workplace an attractive place to be. You can go further and have sign-up incentives exclusive to the episode and within a certain time frame; this gamifies the experienced.

40. Google shopping for recruitment hacked

This may throw you off initially, as you're not selling the position, but in reality you are and there is a way to manifest as a product for sale. Using third party print-on-demand style platforms, you can create t-shirts, mugs, mobile phone protectors and many other types of merchandise, all branded towards the job itself. For example, if the role is junior growth hacker, you can print this with a catchphrase such as "I may be junior, but I aint no junior buddy" with your branding. The secret behind this is that it won't cost you a penny. You will make money if it gets popular, which is a good goal, but the real goal is optimization of the job role. If the job role is kept open year-round, this works even better. In the product description, optimize it with keywords towards your brand and your job opening, including a link to the job opening itself. The goal is to use any real estate opportunities in the merchandising process to signpost links towards your job opening. Remember, it's ok to sell the products too, and you should.

41. LinkedIn

This is the last of the baseline places to search. However, LinkedIn is powerful. Aside from a straightforward search, here are some other assets in the platform to search in:

1. **Groups** - they are powerful places where people share ideas and resources and being part of them will help you find the right growth hacker

2. **Articles** - written by growth hackers about their experience, ideas and other resources; they can give you a window into their thinking and skills
3. **Post Content** – a search can help you find micro-level content on growth hacking being shared or created by growth hackers

The most obvious is a people search. Here are some alternative titles to be used to find a growth hacker:

1. growth hacker
2. growth marketing
3. growth director
4. growth manager
5. growth marketer
6. chief marketing officer
7. vice president growth
8. growth hacking
9. growth hacking director
10. growth hacking CEO
11. growth hacking marketing
12. growth hacking vp
13. growth hacking manager
14. growth hacking founder

These queries will bring you a wide range of people. The key is to dig deeper into their skills, their resources and history. We will leave the deeper dive for another article.

42. LinkedIn introduction recruitment outreach

This is simple, but has a twist. You can go direct but, instead, try using a mutual contact to make the introduction. As strange as this might sound compared to going direct, it's all about how you channel the introduction. The secret to this is to state your interest in the background of that person, looking for good skills, and a potential match to a very lucrative job opening. The reason for this is that the introducer will pre-pitch the opportunity without knowing anything about it. This is because they are interested in bringing good news and value and want to be that person in their network who does this. Let them create that initial soft landing. The copy you use is vital, so craft it carefully with the objective of identifying that important person; you want them and the introduction is very important.

43. LinkedIn posts for recruitment

Beyond what LinkedIn may offer as part of its own recruitment solutions, using 'direct to action' content is key. It's important to have frequent campaigns that not only attract growth hackers, but also allow others to mention, tag, and share with others. This may be basic, but as part of a series of other activities, this will give you a boost into other more assertive measures. Take this next level, tap into some other activities such as growth mentors or other well-known growth hackers get them involved in sharing, commenting and even sponsoring them as part of your advertising campaign. Visibility is key but also memorable and that is something that usually isn't done very well. Memorability means getting very creative with your ad-copy and concept. Although this may be a professional network, this is all the more reason to step outside the norms and get creative. Keep in mind that the same people using LinkedIn are using Tiktok, Instagram, YouTube, and Facebook, where more creative content is being served. The secret behind working with the free and low-cost features in LinkedIn goes beyond their paid re-cruitment solutions. The concept is not to use their recruitment solutions, but to go beyond them.

44. LinkedIn outreach for recruitment referrals

There is no shortage of recruiters on LinkedIn. The power of LinkedIn is that they are easy to find. Create a dedicated and ongoing campaign to recruit the recruiters themselves. There are a few programs to develop, one-offs, ongoing programs, and a more advanced program. This allows you to have flexible entry points for different recruiters to make money and bring you the best candidates. Keep this low friction, but also present the money-making income generation opportunity to widen your reach, to get the best recruiters onboard as well. The secret behind this is not just to find interested recruiters who are willing to be part of your program, but also to target active recruiters in other firms. This will take more creative and careful maneuvering, of course, but this is where you tap into the networks of already active recruiters in competing firms. This means they would be more into your one-off program. To make this work you have to be one step removed. In other words, set up your own identity that doesn't relate to your firm directly so there is no direct conflict or visible conflict of interest.

45. LinkedIn profile baiting

This might throw you off a bit, but it works. It may be questionable, so use your best judgment on how to do this. Create 5-10 key profiles of the ideal candidates you want on your growth team. Detail the profile comprehensively of what you want. Start following like-minded candidates, and the algorithm will help you with this. Get those profiles to develop the network of growth hackers; you want to be seen as peers rather than recruiters or anything else. Once this is set up and you have built a network of who you want, have your recruiter reach out to your baiting profiles and ask for an intro-duction, stating there is an interest in hiring them. Get the baiting profile to reach out to that potential candidate and show them a screenshot or a forward of the introduction request.

46. LinkedIn profile baiting targeting

Building on LinkedIn baiting, use official recruitment posting to men-tion the target candidate in the comments. The reason is you need a few baiting profiles, so if the target is mentioned more than once – ideally, 2-3 times – by completely different and unconnected bait-ing profiles, the candidate pays attention. The secret behind this is to start with the target candidate in mind, then bring in 3-4 more profiles also mentioned in the comments. This way, the target can-didate sees several competing candidates being flagged and this drives urgency.

47. LinkedIn Feature link to dedicated hiring page

The Features function on the platform is a visible feature to give pri-ority above the fold. This will differ by account and type of location in the platform used. However, it's there to be used and that is ex-actly what you need to do. Some of the features to use include di-rect recruitment features, spotlighting top performers, and recruiting recruiters, as part of your referral program. Do not keep your fea-tures static. Update them visually, and copy every 45-60 on an an-nual rotation. This is one of the most valuable pieces of real estate on LinkedIn and has to be used wisely, so rotations and consis-tency are key to ensuring attention is sustained.

48. LinkedIn Live events

There are two types of events you can set up. Direct ones are for recruitment; the second is not related to recruitment but targeting your potential recruits. For direct recruitment events, have an annual calendar with pre-set event registration landing pages. Keep this consistent, even if you're not actively hiring. It's a great way to warm up potential candidates for future open positions. The indirect events can be about growth hacking; for example, hosting a growth hacking expert. The idea is that the topic will attract those in the space who want to participate. Once you get them registered, your direct recruitment hit list is automatically ready to go. The secret behind this is consistency, tapping into a wider network and getting the direct contacts of your direct recruits and potential future recruits. This can also be used as a way to recruit recruiters who can work on referral programs. You would need to pre-screen registration to ensure you have the right people for this event.

49. LinkedIn groups tapped and cross-pollinated

Find, join and engage relevant groups. That part is simple, but how to use those groups is the key. First and foremost, don't join low engagement and sleepy groups. Find the most active ones and join those. When you start, use your first post to introduce yourself and state you recruit growth hackers and are here to add value to the group. This is the first and non-spam opportunity you get to make a first impression, so make it shine. Add in resources such as a recent report with something that adds value fast. Start looking for questions or interesting posts to respond to; focus on the latest 12-15 of them. State that you're new, and activate your participation in the message so they know. Start contributing weekly with data, facts, resources, cases and even asking questions to get insights and inputs. Ideally, find 10-12 groups and cross-pollinate your efforts so that you're using your efforts multiple times across all of them. If you find a good question or comment in one group, bring it over to the others, and so on. The secret behind this is widening your network within relevant groups and focusing on the active ones. Make efforts once, and spread them across the groups without it being spam or seen as a way to distribute your efforts. Use this as a forum to engage them in your growth hacking practices, but also be clear of your recruiting all the time. Finally, enroll the group admin into your recruitment referral program as an income generation opportunity. This may be sensitive; hence, good judgment needs to be applied with regard to who and how to do this.

50. LinkedIn keep track and engaged

Follow, link, and comment on a wide range of potential candidates and keep adding new ones all the time. Keep the comments light, simple and positive. This approach is indirect but very obvious and there is nothing wrong with it. You will need to apply good judgment in term of who you do this with, for how long, and what comments you use. The idea is to place yourself top-of-mind with little effort by automating this process. The secret behind this is to always keep expanding the network of who you follow, track and engage, and keep it consistent (automation). Although this might be a light-touch approach, this creates a soft landing for future direct messages for recruitment purposes. Finally, it would be a good idea, to create a recruitment profile for your company on LinkedIn and use that account for these efforts.

51. LinkedIn InMail: a surefire way it inboxes

One of the lowest cost advertising options provided by LinkedIn is InMail. The potential for LinkedIn targeting and profiling companies with InMail is powerful. This is because LinkedIn has a very good spam score and can enter anyone's inbox with few barriers. They are also always current on contact details. Although many of the other hacks are free, this paid approach is well worth it. It's low cost, effective, and well targeted. Use InMail for direct recruitment purposes only. The only exception to the rule is if you're not actively hiring but want to warm-up candidates; then, use your other hacks such as an open coffee day, an event or award as a hook to engage them.

52. Community deep dive

Communities have a lot of hidden talent. They are there to learn and get support from, including access to resources. People do not think of communities as a way to get a job. Hence, this gives a big competitive advantage to tapping into communities of growth hackers.

53. Joining a growth hacker community

Can't find them? Join them. **Growth hacking communities** have sprung up, from Reddit to Discord. They are not all the same, and not of great quality. However, leaving quality aside, you never know who you will find in those deep dark corners where no one else is looking. Here is a list of a few:

1. GrowthHackers
2. Inbound.org
3. Quibb
4. Reddit's Growth Hacking Subreddit
5. Growth Hacker TV
6. Growth Hacker Talk
7. HubbleHQ
8. Facebook

Beyond this, perform searches in Discord for growth hacking communities and even in Telegram on their open search. These communities want to recruit and hence make themselves discoverable.

54. Bring the best data to get engagement and new ideas

One of the best ways to add value to a community is learning and there's no better way than data. Bring in simple, high impact and meaningful data. Use both public data and data you have generated. The more original the data, the better. The secret behind this is to trigger a conversation, such as validation, new perspectives, alternatives, implications, and new ideas. Drive the narrative into those directions to get engagement. This enables you to find the most active participants, and those who have high impact participation. Using that pool, you can directly recruit them or tap into them for recruitment referrals.

55. Bring the best hacks to drive new ideas

Use your existing hacks to drive engagement. This can be ones you have executed or one you want feedback on before executing. Creating a series of posts or comments can be very useful to convert the hack into a storyline. Think of this like a play-by-play approach to trickle engagement. The idea is to create engagement. The secret here is to identify active participants and recruit them, or look for for recruitment referrals.

56. Bring the best problems to attract talent

Get them solving a growth problem. Tell it as a story and in the form of a series and get the community involved. This is a crowdsourcing approach to engage the audience. This can be taken one step further by giving prizes or other incentives with the success of a solution – and do not overlook runner-up incentives too. The secret behind this is that the top minds are attracted to the most challenging problems to be cracked. They are the ones you want to hire. The good news is that they will also know others like them, so you can tap into that as well for recruitment referrals.

57. Bring the best mentors to drive the narrative

Bring external mentors who are not part of the community to participate. In fact, if you belong to several communities, it would be best
to hire a mentor and have him or her participate in your format over
all the communities at once. The idea is to bring and sponsor other
expertise that those in the community would not normally have access to. This brings a new thinking, but also taps into other networks. The secret behind this is leveraging several communities
and using the expert and influential power of the mentor to get
higher engagement across the communities under your brand. This
will enable your recruitment drive to get more active member insight
for direct and referral recruitment.

58. Enrich communities via cross-pollination

Leverage your access points across several communities. Ideally, if
you are part of 10-12 communities, you can bring in ideas or conversations from elsewhere to communities that do not have the
same. This way, you can source and user-generate your content to
drive the narrative in your direction. This is great for also tapping
into what is really on the minds of people in the growth community
in a relevant and timely fashion. In fact, you can synchronize your
conversations and trigger the narrative by quoting from other communities. The secret behind this is putting in less effort, tapping into
what is current and relevant and using this to control the narrative.
This allows you to identify the most active participants and recruit
them directly or source referral recruitments.

59. Create and bring a new thread or topic

Don't just join in, find new hot topics or problems being solved and
create a topic, a threat or a subthread, depending on the structure
of the community. Own a domain in a growth hacking community,

ideally something pressing, of interest and a niche not well covered in the community. The secret behind this is to tap into a niche not covered, own the conversation, and drive interest towards working with your company.

60. Create a growth hacker community

Create your own growth hacker community with a twist. Make it around your industry specifically and promote resources provided by your company. In fact, you can go further and get your growth team to run this, and use this for a few reasons. One is for generating new ideas, validating experiments, finding new hacks and finally getting new hires.

61. Center a community around a set of problems

This is all about finding the best minds to work with. Identify 10 long-term growth challenges that are common across many organizations. Bring content by putting data behind them, such as implications, consequences, alternatives and trends. This enables a narrative to drive understanding and interest, but more importantly a reason to be part of the solution by agreeing on the problem and its mechanics. The secret behind this is that the brightest minds are attracted to the most challenging problems. This would first and foremost serve as a crowdsourcing approach to helping solve your own growth issue in your organization and then identifying the top minds in the conversation and recruiting them.

62. Create niche growth hacking communities

Focus on 10-12 niche growth hacking related topics, such as outreach, content strategy, growth tools, growth experiments, growth talent etc. Focused topic themed communities help you organize talent by areas your own organization wants to develop. This enables your organization to be at the center of creating solutions and get others around those solutions and to keep developing on them. The secret behind this is to identify your growth long-term development challenges, align and build external communities around them. This enables you to identify the best talent possible and recruit them.

63. Create an educational community

Take your 10-12 focus areas for growth-related topics, and enrich those communities with training and education. Focus on micro-training content. This can be optimized by sourcing the best talent, inputting data and testing their ideas and putting together training and education to help the community advance their thinking and influence the narrative. The secret behind this is solving your own long-term growth challenges while crowdsourcing ideas and expertise, and then hiring them.

64. Create a gamified community

Take the niche and educational approach and gamify the experience. Create levels, badges, points etc to reward those who actively participate and take this one step further by having a weekly top 10 ranking of participants. This can be applied and overlaid to other communities as well to gamify the experience and gain access to other communities and bring them to yours. The secret behind this is keeping top talent engaged once you identify who they are, and this challenges emerging talent to work harder. Do not forget to offer prizes and other incentives on a frequent basis.

65. Advanced growth hacking community

A gated community for advanced growth hacking that combines both topics of data and education. This can be a paid community to filter including pre-qualifications. This builds a club in which the best minds can come together. The secret behind this is nurturing the best talent and watching them progress until you can hire them. This can also serve as a crowd sourcing platform for your own internal growth team to work with.

66. Create a growth hacking trends community

The power of trends is getting people ahead of the curve. Cover new trends, those that are emerging and past trends and where they have gone. Cover them thoroughly with as many examples and data to help others understand those growth hacking trends. The secret behind this is fear of missing out. More or less trends mean change and if you don't see or seize them, you're behind. Play this role with growth hacking trends.

67. Sponsor a growth hacker community

Once you've found a community or two of growth hackers you like, sponsor them, whether it be a report, some unique content or even an event. This gives you a voice and literally the ability to state that you're hiring. This should be an ongoing and long-term approach.

68. Sponsor an event to get sign-ups

Simply sponsor minor events as a low-friction and low-cost approach to spend the least possible money to get access to the sign-ups. Leverage your products, services and network to have previous, current and future sign-ups access them. The secret behind this is creating a financial incentive as an additional revenue stream for the community, based on recruitment referral payouts.

69. Sponsor a micro-competition to find top talent

Sponsor a micro-competition in the community. This is a quick, simple and meaningful growth hacking competition. This can be a best-ranked experiment or growth hacking idea, or even a best performing growth hack. The secret behind this is to keep it small and frequent. This gives you visibility on active members and those who have a great interest towards solving problems.

70. Sponsor spotlighting of top talent for inspiration

Profile top talent and sponsor their exposure in the community. The secret behind this is to simply get others inspired. Using a direct call to action for recruitment can work very well with this approach if positioned effectively.

71. Sponsor courses and bring them in

Source external top quality growth hacking courses, give an incentive for sign-up with bonuses and place it in the community exclusively for members only. The secret behind this is leveraging education and interest in personal development growth, and capturing the contact details. Enrich that data, and directly target for recruitment.

72. Sponsor a roundtable to solve common problems

Leverage access to several communities and host a roundtable that is used across all communities at once. The effort is made once, but it can be used across several communities at once. The purpose of the roundtable is to focus on an economic problem, get the top thinkers around the problem and drive a conversation around it.

The secret behind this is driving an interesting, relevant and very compelling narrative that attracts the top minds in growth hacking.

73. Sponsor a growth hacking hero

Find a very talented growth hacker, and back them in the community. Use this as an opportunity to use the influence of a major player in the community to work on your behalf. Back them with resources, ideas, data and even access to products and services they can use to stimulate influence towards your brand. The secret behind this is finding a very influential player in the community who can be sponsored and can drive your agenda for recruiting the best talent. Also, offer them referral revenue for recruits they bring in.

74. Advertise on a growth hacker community

Don't want to waste time with sponsorship? Advertise outright. In fact, they wont charge much as they don't have many companies chasing their community for exposure. For a very low cost and over a good period of time, you can secure direct recruitment placements within communities themselves.

75. Advertise open positions

Openly advertise vacant positions in the community. There are a few ways of optimizing this. First, integrate the ad with hot topics in the community. Another way is to encourage the community owners to go beyond the ad by giving them a small but meaningful kickback on recruitment success. The secret behind this is direct recruitment without wasting time.

76. Advertise passive positions

Always have vacant positions to build your database. This allows you to continuously use automation tools to filter and qualify and keep a warmed-up database of potential results ready to go. The secret behind this is continuous visibility and interest in top talent. This builds your database and keeps you current and relevant.

77. Advertise open coffee days

Advertise an open coffee day. An open coffee day is where you bring your top decision-makers, physically and virtually, and your growth team for an informal gathering for 30-60 minutes to get to know each other. The purpose is a soft-landing to break the ice between future recruits and top decision makers. The secret behind this is that talent is attracted to getting access to the top decision-makers and being heard. This can be leveraged easily in the relationship through the open coffee day approach.

78. Advertise a meet-the-growth-team day

Going beyond an open coffee day approach, make it more focused and keep it exclusively with your growth team. The informal process not only breaks the ice but also allows for more in-depth technical questions and an opportunity for talent to see the growth team culture in action. The secret behind this is direct exposure to the growth team at the same time to see culture and personality fit.

79. Advertise intern and apprentice positions

Don't have an open position yet? Advertise your intern or apprentice programs. Leverage past interns and apprentices with their video testimonials. Focus the messaging on their concerns about joining, and how that was overcome, then how they managed to grow and now how it's a place where they thrive. The secret behind this is that a storyline helps walk future talk through a journey they can relate to.

80. Hackathons and competitions

Find the best talent by showing them their best talent. There is no better way than a competition or a show-and-tell environment.

81.. Make a competition

Creating and promoting your own competition puts a case into play. In other words, give a scenario in which you have a scorecard system and this enables you to find the best. In fact, this should not be a one-off, but rather an ongoing yearly program.

82. Monthly growth hacking hackathons

Engage the community for the best talent to emerge through a competition. Make this competition lucrative for participants. It's not just about being number one, or a runner-up but rather include incentives. The secret behind this is making this frequent, and making it viral by ensuring its share. Use small content pieces where you have moments of brilliance to push via social media and via the competitors and the audience who follows.

83. Drop it into growth communities

Take your competition and recruit directly from growth hacking communities and groups but also share content related to progress, outcomes, results and major learnings. This becomes a way to deliver value to growth hacking communities and groups, a way to attract talent and grow your recruitment pool. The secret behind this is being able to widen your recruitment pool by engaging the best talent to participate in your competition.

84. Big prizes, with runner-up gamification

Incentivize the whole competition, from interest, entry, participation and outcomes. Gamify the process, and include gamifying and incentivizing those who watch to share the competition with others to expand the reach. The secret behind this is not always about having big prizes but rather having many prizes along the way that keep everyone in the process engaged.

85. Winner scores a job with prizes

Make the prize the job itself. Very simple, in this case you can be selective on entry requirements but you want to be wide enough to include people who you may overlook but who have great talent. One of the great outcomes is that you may find more than one candidate within this process who might fit other positions coming up or yet to be created. The secret behind this is being very explicit about what you want, making the process fun and transparent. It would be a wise idea to incentivize runner-ups as well with other prizes to keep them engaged.

86. Build an all-star judging panel

Want to attract some amazing talent? Start with an all-star panel of judges. This gives you two advantages: one is having good judges who attract people via their own networks, and using their expertise to enrich your competition. The secret behind this is being able to get the top growth hacking talent outside of your organization involved. Focus on judges who have a well-known track record and those who are willing to participate, help and advance talent. This creates a potent recruitment environment.

87. Set up a demo day

Demo days are the last part of an incubator's or accelerator's cohort. It essentially lets their best talent pitch to investors. If they are good, they will have growth hackers working with them. Like the competition idea? Why not run your own demo day where teams can come up with their own growth hackers. What is interesting, is that you can make them within your scope, such as by industry and even specific market segments to be tackled.

88. Partner with startup accelerators

Don't reinvent the wheel - go to those who have mastered the demo day. The best part is that most demo days are designed for a wide range of participants to be part of their program. The goal is to reach out to the best of those startup accelerators and become part of their program. This can be as simple as a judge appointing someone from your team, or sponsoring the demo day itself. The secret behind this is networking. The startup accelerators have invested in identifying and promoting the best possible talent they have, so use these efforts for your benefit.

89. Go covert - participate in another demo day

Inject your own team with a new idea for a demo day. This is a longer, more involved process, but this enables you to be deep inside the process within the startup accelerators' program. The secret behind this is gaining direct and covert access to key talent you may not otherwise see, just by being involved in the demo day alone. This enables you to find hidden talent that may not be so visible or even spotlight team members. Keep track of startups that do not make it, as they will always have leftover talent seeking new opportunities.

90. Side hustle demo day

Create an add-on to top-up demo day based on already existing ones. This would be a unique feature to add to a demo day in partnership with the startup accelerators. This will need some unique positioning. The goal of a demo day is to attract investment, but you're not investing nor adding to those startups, you're in fact taking their talent. The secret behind this is having a growth hacking add-on with feedback in front of investors for feedback they want as well. This gives the startup an advantage of feedback and being spotlighted at the same time, a unique window into their talent. This gives you access to see who you can recruit. Remember, not all the team members want to be part of those startups for a variety of reasons. Keeping in touch with them, even if they reject the opportunity, is the secret, as if things don't go well, they may be seeking the next opportunity, and this is where you step in.

91. Round-up other demo days

Don't spend time and effort on one demo day, simply round-up the demo days. This covers more ground with better outcomes. Create a blog post to start with featuring the startups across all demo days with their outcomes and list it in such a way that it can be filtered. This important resource can be used by many people. The secret here is reaching out to those startups and showing or telling them about this listing for their benefit and asking them to enrich their own profiles by adding team members. This is where your direct access points to their growth hackers are created. Then, further enrich the data on your end with contact details of the team and get in touch directly with the growth hacker or growth hacking team for recruitment purposes.

92. Cover other demo days as content

For the demo days you do not cover or manage to get to, you can use a round-up style approach but reach out online to populate the content. This way, you can enhance your reach by leveraging your existing round-ups. If you don't have existing round-ups, you can use ethos as an opportunity to start that process. The point is to create a database and enrich that data to access their top talent, at the same time giving them exposure.

93. Sponsor other competitions

Don't want to set up your own competition? Simply be part of an existing competition as a sponsor, which gives you access to the talent. This gives exposure and an ability to have pre-access to talent before they become exposed to the public.

94. Offer an add-on open coffee day

Add on prizes for access to your top decision-makers and growth team. An open coffee day,, whether physical, virtual or hybrid, serves as an informal entry point. This allows potential talent who are motivated to know more about your organization and build their network to join. The secret behind this is finding hidden talent within other networks in an informal format.

95. Sponsor a contender/startup

This might be a bit on edge, but it works. Pick a favorite, regardless of who might win, and simply back them. Sponsor them - it's a lot like a Formula One race. Get your name placed in the competition and this gives you the exposure. In the situation of a demo day, this would also work; you can sponsor a team and get your exposure via their presence and participation. In return for your sponsorship, you will ask for access to contacts and introductions within the competition and beyond. You can build further on this as part of your terms and conditions. The secret to this is turning a competition into a Formula One sponsored event, which has never happened before. It's controversial and that is the whole idea behind it. Controversy creates attention and focus. This controversy needs to be played well and within ethical and decent means to protect your brand. Position it as a unique, bold and creative move.

96. Media asset coverage for sponsorship exchange

Use your own digital media assets in exchange for sponsorship. Give this a high value and use this as the sponsorship package. In the sense of media assets, this would cover things like email newsletters, transaction emails, email signatures, social media posts and bios, website placements etc. The secret behind this is to leverage space you already have with an audience to show your sponsorship and leverage that for exposure inside a startup accelerator as a supporter. In return, you can leverage direct contact details within the cohort, both previous and current and other exposure points. The idea is to tap into networks you don't have access to and identify hidden growth hacking talent within them.

97. Sponsor a segment with prizes

Don't want to sponsor the whole cohort, competition or program? Focus on a segment that is growth hacking-related, either directly or indirectly. If they have something growth-themed, they will tap into that only. With that sponsorship, you can give a smaller prize since it's a segment not a whole cohort, competition or program. This can be, for example, a cohort's growth training session and support component. The secret to this is direct and explicit exposure to their growth team. You can take this further and offer further

Let's hire the best talent

This exercise helps identify the best hacks to hire talent. This enables you to track performance, re-use top performers, discard poor performers, and create new hacks that might outperform existing ones. Choose hacks you want to use. Write down the number and name of the hack. Once a hack is applied, capture top-level learning points and the result.

Hack | # | Name of hacked
Learning | | What did you learn?
Result | | What are the results?

Hack | # | Name of hacked
Learning | | What did you learn?
Result | | What are the results?

Hack | # | Name of hacked
Learning | | What did you learn?
Result | | What are the results?

Hack | # | Name of hacked
Learning | | What did you learn?
Result | | What are the results?

Hack | # | Name of hacked
Learning | | What did you learn?
Result | | What are the results?

Performance of hacks

Capture, top, and poor performance hiring hacks here. At the same time, generate new hacks by combing existing hiring hacks or using existing hacks to inspire a new hiring hack. Use this performance page to develop your next action plan with your team to outperform your competition in finding, attracting, and retaining top growth talent.

Top performing Hacks

Hack | # | Name of hacked

Hack | # | Name of hacked

Hack | # | Name of hacked

Poor performing Hacks

Hack | # | Name of hacked

Hack | # | Name of hacked

Hack | # | Name of hacked

New Combo Hacks

Hack | # | Name of hacked | # | Name of hacked

Hack | # | Name of hacked | # | Name of hacked

Hack | # | Name of hacked | # | Name of hacked

New generated hacks

Hack | # | Name of hacked

Hack | # | Name of hacked

Hack | # | Name of hacked

exposure via your own networks, but with the caveat of them sharing everything within their own networks. This helps expand beyond the direct access points within the cohort itself. Ask the accelerator or organizer also for past contacts to tap into them as well, beyond the current ones you're targeting.

98. Product placement as a sponsorship lever

Use the value of your products and services so that they can give these away to their direct audience and beyond as a sponsorship value, rather than paying for it. This can be a light and powerful way to cover more demo days and other startup accelerators or any other program without having to invest heavily. The secret to this is getting a wider spread of exposure and access without having to invest more time and effort. This also gives you the advantage of learning which channels are best performing to gain recruitment leads, and then deepening your sponsorship programs with them specifically.

99. Partner to create a competition

Don't want to create or sponsor? Then partner with someone. Co-create a growth hacking competition and use this to source the talent from the deep dark corners where you're not able to see or find the top growth hackers.

100. Co-prizes and runner-up gamification

Do not give away alone; bring in others with you and then gamify it. The approach here is to also use others' resources with yours to make attractive runner-up prizes. The goal here is to make more attractive prizes; to make it fun but also to gain a wider access point. The secret behind this is a lower cost, low friction, high impact approach to tapping deeper into competitions and the like for a wider audience, without having to invest more time and effort but getting high impact at the same time.

101. Niche down with key players

Don't waste your time once you have pinpointed the most effective channels. Double down and niche down at the same time. Examples include focusing on FinTech growth or Digital health growth. This way, you are able to gain even more impact and continue to go deeper within those niches. The secret behind this is sectoral focus points where you're able to gain access to growth hackers by sector for your own development purposes. Keep in mind, the best growth hackers are cross-functional and this might be a way to tap into deeper tech skills and top up their training internally later on to make them more cross-functional.

102. Develop micro competitions

Don't create this but partner with those who have volume and access to growth hackers. Develop an annual competition with them but on a micro level. The secret behind this is that micro works. Small, bite-size competitions attached to bigger ones can be used as runner-up placements, or other incentives, of course. The micro competition is designed to be small, quick and fun. This way, you can gain access to a large audience quickly to identify hidden growth hacking talent.

103. Create a rotating partnership

Don't do this once. Create an annual calendar and have other partners filling the gap with time slots. This way, you get ongoing development across a different set of partners. The secret behind this is leveraging others' competitions efforts and reaching into other competitions. This basically positions you as the facilitator and allows you to leverage all sides.

104. Partners who need you the most

Find companies in more traditional industries with a more traditional business model and approach but with a mindset where they want to tap into new thinking. The secret behind this is to get them access to growth hackers and growth hacking strategies they would not normally have and build a competition around it.

105. Participate in demo days

Thinking back to demo days: if you don't want to create your own, join one. Although the purpose may be different, like fundraising, you can use this as a form of access to networks. You can network with the startups and their teams to identify top talent.

106. Participate as a spectator on a demo day

Very simple, keep things light and low friction. Melt into the audience and use that opportunity to network covertly, rather than out and upfront. This has a drawback of widening your network but on the other hand it helps you narrow down and focus on quality connections. Hack this by using a recruitment card, which is a card that says you're hiring, and pay bounty fees for referrals. Second, directly ask growth experts for referrals in their network as you meet different people.

107. Participate as a judge on a demo day

Another simple approach. Widen your exposure at the demo day (or similar), by being a judge. Announce your position as judge via the host's network and make it part of the conditions of participation. Use your one network as well. As demo day arrives, the startup accelerator will be driving its network to learn how they will be doing this for optimal placement to ensure your participation is known and promoted. The secret behind this is to use the growth perspective on the judge panel to get more interest from the audience. Capturing the audience may be challenging as a judge alone, hence you may request a mentoring session prior to or after the demo day itself, or a meet and greet session but by registration only. This way, you're able to directly network, have contact details and use a recruitment card. A recruitment card contains your details with a big message saying 'We are hiring' to allow both direct and referral bounty payments for referral recruitments.

108. Announce participation at demo day

Generate a larger network by announcing your organization's participation at a demo day using your network, and social media platforms. This provides support to the demo day but also indicates to your audience that you will be there for networking purposes. The secret behind this is being in one place at one time but having many people come to you. It's simple, but works to attract the right audience of people. Carry a recruitment card with you; this is essentially your details but for recruitment purposes only. This may be a very direct approach but it's the best way to leverage this opportunity. At the same time, referral bounty fees are paid on the card. This way, if someone knows someone they know they ever get for their referrals.

109. Go live via LinkedIn

LinkedIn live business content is dry. Go live and bring it to life, by being the only one who streams the demo day via LinkedIn. Alongside this, have your team on the chat providing text commentary as the streaming takes place. This gives a third dimension to the experience. Posting the completed video, and using a sign-up link in advance, allows you to re-target the same audience by sending the video with an in-depth article written by your team. This gives you the ability to drive your 'call to actions' in the streaming by your team, in the article when published. The recorded video can be edited with the call to action in it. The secret behind this is to use those placements of 'call to action' to directly recruit growth hackers watching and following.

110. Surrogate participation via streaming

Go one step further, and take the approach of having a POC (point of view) converge but streamed. This can be done with play-by-play comments and analysis. The secret behind this is building an audience in advance and tapping into the audience in a unique way. This allows you to capture their contact details to register for this streaming coverage. This then enables you to comment from a growth perspective to get comments and use the database of contact to reach out to them for direct and indirect recruitment campaigns.

111. Mentorship and coaching

Not all growth hackers work in the same way. More experienced and broader skilled growth hackers will be mentoring or even coaching. Mentoring is giving advice from experience, while coaching is helping someone to find the answers via their own process.

112. Find a growth mentor

There are some mentor networks already set up such as Growth Mentor and other sub-communities within LinkedIn and Facebook. The point is, you can hire them for an hour, give them a specific problem and see how they solve it. If you like it, hire them, and don't ask for another mentor. Remember, a mentor is someone with experience who gives advice to you whereas a coach uses a process to help you find your own solutions.

113. Celebrity mentor event

Find a well-known growth hacker or entrepreneur who has been growth hacking. Get them to become a mentor and have them guide future recruits as a way to attract them. Run events and community platforms around them to acquire and retain an ongoing flow of interest. The secret behind this is to attract top talent but also to engage them over the long term, whether you have an active vacancy or not. This is also an excellent testing ground for new ideas and seeing talent in action.

114. Sponsored mentorship for future growth hackers

Run a sponsorship program to match up future recruits with mentors. The mentors, being experienced in growth hacking, can use a structured scoring system to help rank and identify future talent. The secret behind this is giving value to future growth hackers, getting them engaged and having a way to identify and prioritize hires using the expertise of mentors.

115. Mentor ranking and recognition

Find, score and rank growth mentors external to your organization. Keep this frequent and categorized to identify several segments. The secret behind this is engaging mentors into your programs and eventually getting them into a recruitment referral program or even potentially hiring them.

116. Mentors behind powerful companies

Find mentors who have been behind the scenes of very popular companies. Recognize them where others have not. Doing this enables you to tap into their expertise and pay them for inputs into your own efforts. The secret behind this is either directly recruiting them or having them refer recruits to you directly for direct compensation.

117. Mentor network partnerships

Find growth mentor networks and partner with them. Tap into their network and actively recruit growth mentors directly as well as operating a referral program. The secret to this is giving compensation to the mentor network as another form of revenue stream.

118. Find a growth coach

A coach is someone who has a process they use for you to find the solutions. Finding someone like this would be interesting to test them out for an hour or two. This helps you see their thought process so you can either hire them or get a referral. Remember, a coach uses a process to help you find your own solutions whereas a mentor is someone with experience who advises you.

119. Growth coach service

Set up your own growth coaching service in the form of a market-place. This enables you to tap into the whole market and gain data on what is happening. More importantly, it self-funds your efforts in finding talent. This works by having a scoring system on both ends and ranking them, including reviews etc. The secret to this is to identify both coaches and coaches' talent to recruit.

120. Growth coach ranking

Rank external coaches into top ten rankings using 10-12 different categories. This gives you a wide range of growth coaches to rank. Remember, these are coaches who help their clients find the an-swers and usually use their own tools. The secret behind this is tap-ping into their methods and effective usage of those methods. Find those who can use those methods best and recruit them.

121. Growth coach events

Host periodic growth coaching events sponsored by your organiza-tion. The secret behind this is tapping into the wider growth hacking community. By doing so, this provides the ability to identify and re-cruit top talent. This also serves as a method to collect contact in-formation and set up automated emailing campaigns to keep them engaged and eventually work their way towards direct recruitment.

122. Growth coach recruitment referral program

Overtly recruit growth coaches to recruit for you as a passive in-come opportunity. The secret behind this is utilizing the coaches' networks and skills to identify and filter talent. Ensure they do this exclusively with your organization. This means compensation and support systems that keep them comfortable but also support their success. This can be integrated into other recruitment referral programs to cover more ground.

123. Growth coach recruitment standalone event

Sponsor coaches who have their own events as part of a recruitment referral program. They can use their content and network to attract their audience and then use this as a recruitment channel. Be sure to align compensation with performance in an attractive format so coaches can run several of these events.

124. Ask a mentor for a growth hacker

Aside from finding a direct growth mentor, you may want to network with other types of mentors who can find you growth mentors as well. Mentors who are involved in scaling startups or leadership development might just know someone you cannot see or find, so ask them.

125. Top-ranked mentor growth hacks

Get mentors to design and share their own growth hacks with full credit to them. The idea is to use scoring systems so you can rank them. Use a wide range of categories to have several growth hacks. The secret behind this is to get mentors to share their experience and attract recruits who would be interested in using those growth hacks. Potentially, they can advance those growth hacks for credit for their inputs. The secret behind this is community building and using this to attract top recruits.

126. Get a mentor to run a live growth hack

Sponsor a mentor and have them run a growth hack live. Run these events and stream them on social media live functions. This should be by registration only to capture contact information. If you can, provide a unique portion of the event only for registered users right away, like a question and answer session. The secret behind this is to engage mentors who are growth experts to build an audience of growth hackers you can recruit from.

127. Get a mentor to run a growth hacking mentorship group

Further build community and mentole it by using membership to pay for operations of the community, including compensating mentors. The secret behind this is having commitment from your community by knowing they are invested in their own progress and truly interested in learning. Once you have a captive audience of those interested in learning and development, you have a potent recruitment pool to choose from.

128. Mentor top advice email newsletter

Gather your top growth mentors, both internal and external, and create a weekly email newsletter. The goal is flow of unique and practical content on a frequent basis. The secret behind this is to position and place recruitment positions that are open to that mailing list; these can also be used to deploy a recruitment referral program.

129. Set up a LinkedIn mentorship group

Tap into the power of professional networks with LinkedIn. Use their group feature to bring in qualified growth mentors into a wider and more public forum for supporting mentorship for growth. By doing this, you're able to tap into new networks but also identify top talent. The secret behind this is using the power of LinkedIn to identify talent at the top of your funnel and then filtering from this group to find direct recruits and those who can help with recruitment within your referral program.

130. Ask a mentor to mentor a growth hacker for 60 days

Pair up good growth mentors with growth hackers you plan to hire. As an incentive when hiring, give new growth hackers 60 days' mentorship from external growth hackers who can guide them in their new role. The secret behind this is to attract talent with high profile mentors, supporting them in the role, and scaffolding their success internally. It would be a good idea to record this as well in the form of short videos and use this as part of your marketing to attract new talent.

131. Ask a coach for a growth hacker

Likewise, a general coach or someone with a background in startup development and leadership may know someone you can't find. Ask them and get the referral and do not be shy in compensating them for a successful hire.

132. Growth coach new methods tried and tested

Get new potential recruits to test out new ideas from coaches and use this as a ranking system to filter through and identify talent. Be sure to have an incentivized system to compensate coaches and potentially their coaches.

133. Growth coach recruitment referral program

As with the other recruitment programs, have one dedicated to growth coaches. Ensure it's exclusive with the best support for their success. At the same time, tailor this to the needs of growth coaches as well. This might also include growth hacks such as providing them with your own assessment tools which they can brand as their own, or licensed power users for their clients.

134. Growth coach for featuring their top coaches

As part of other support programs for growth coaches for recruitment, you can give coaches the power to nominate their best students. This can be incentivized both for the student and the coach. This gives the coaches another tool but also a bigger incentive to recruit and to do the filtering for you in advance.

135. Growth coach sponsored media assets

Sponsor your coaches' media assets, such as their social media bios, email signatures, newsletters or anywhere else that they have visibility to the general public. Combined with other recruitment referral programs and incentives, this can be very powerful in supporting their success and income generation with your referral program. The secret behind this is tapping indirectly into their audience, but giving them the revenue for filtering and closing.

136. Create growth coach mastermind

Get the best growth coaches you can find and build a mastermind to cultivate the best of this type of talent. The purpose is to get peer-to-peer mentoring to help members solve their problems with input and advice from the other group members. This can become a very powerful platform for your organization beyond recruitment.

This can serve as a powerful source of new ideas, insights and even identification of very lucrative trends. The secret behind this is the power of this group but also enabling them to help your organization with its ongoing recruitment requirements.

137. Attract them with some bait

What if they are looking for you but there is no way for them to know you're looking for them? This is a longer-term strategy but it's less effort overall as it lasts for a long time. This gives you a wider net to work with and truly find top talent growth hackers.

138. Growth hacking articles

Write growth hacking articles, that are SEO, to have growth hackers interact by communicating with their solutions or inputs. Do not educate them on what they know but rather bring them into the problem-solving process.

139. Write the article for them

No effort, all the credit. A magic formula that always works. Develop periodical content, ideally on a weekly basis. Start with a blog article post. Find a growth hacker you want to hire, and ask them to give feedback on this article. State that you would like to attribute this article to them as the author. Promote this blog post, and allow them to use their network to share and promote it as well. Get them involved in more than one article and aim to have at least 15-20 different growth hackers you do this with. The secret behind this is creating a large volume of content that is meaningful, tapping into the expertise of the growth hacker, and building a relationship with that growth hacker. The goal is to make them look good, and want to be part of your company.

140. Repurposing articles into more content

Going one step beyond, if you have created an article you have put a growth hacker's name to, reuse it. Take that blog article and convert it into audio-format, a slide-show, a video, or a series of social media posts. Do not overlook short-form content methods such as TikTok and YouTube shorts as a series of videos that link long content. You can also create infographics or other visual aids that stand alone but promote the single post. The secret behind this is to expand your single point of efforts into several outcomes to tap into different audience content consumption preferences. This enables you to utilize the networks of the growth hackers you have featured to attract them toward your company.

141. Give them a piece of an article

Create long-form list style content. Rather than just one growth hacker per article, you can loop several of them into a single article by giving them a single piece within that article. This also can be used as a round-up style piece of content, where you take all the single articles and put them into a larger single article in which the other articles are mentioned. This is great for repurposing, but also creating more exposure. The secret behind this is being creative with existing content to stretch its shelf-life, at the same time increasing exposure. This will help in tapping into the broader network of top growth hackers for recruitment purposes.

142. Give them a platform

Beyond being part of an article, create a profile for them on your company blog and on your website. This allows you to SEO. The optimization of exposure gives a few benefits. First, it shows diversity of quality content for your own brand. Second, it shows your depth of reach into experts in the growth hacking fields. Third, it expands your network. The secret here is tying your target recruit into your brand from the start without any commitment. Consider it as being like an internship; without it being one, it's close enough to get them interested in your organization.

143. Add them to an old article

Don't want to create a lot of new content, or want to test this hack before expanding on it? Go back to older articles and update the content; when doing so, add in those growth hackers as part of the content. The secret behind this is if your content is already performing, you utilize existing traffic and interest. This gives the growth hacker you're attracting to contribute a much better entry point of confidence in your organization and its intentions.

144. Roundtable opinion pieces

Create an article that is an interview of several growth hackers giving their opinions on one topic. This way, you can target several potential hires at the same time and get their opinions in comparison to one another. The secret behind this is to promote this article and give them exposure and show the growth community your active role in driving talent. At the same time, this is a way to develop rapport with key opinion-makers and recruit them.

145. Social media posts

Take those articles and create a series of social media posts. Use the comments features in the network to identify those who have an interest in solving the problems you present in the article. Do not be shy to use YouTube and Tiktok; you might be surprised who you might find there.

146. Give them a take-over

Give a day or half-day take-over on your social media platform. This usually would be within the stories function in any of the major platforms. The goals is to show a day in the life of a growth hacker. This form of exposure drives interest but does something bigger: it gets the growth hacker pre-engaged in your organization's development in a very light and easy format. The secret behind this is content creation that shows your brand confidence in attracting, promoting and working with the world's best talent. This drives attention, but also opens up several networks where hidden talent is available.

147. Series of short interviews

Develop a top-10 format style of interviews. For example "Top 10 growth hacking success stories". This can be a very easy series of content stories to promote and gain attention with. This again promotes talent you want to hire, or talent like them you would like to hire. This gives your audience and theirs a signal of what you're looking for. The secret behind this is almost like having a checklist of what you're looking for as an end goal in the form of stories. They can be used as part of your talent attraction videos and other materials as well.

148. Feature top performers

Feature your internal top performers in a series of posts on how to succeed as a growth hacker. This will serve as an indirect criteria checklist of what you would be looking for from talent you're about to hire. The secret behind this is demonstrating success through the talent you have cultivated at your organization. By doing so, those who would like to be part of your organization get a cheatsheet to understand what would be required to work at your organization. Use this for both direct recruitment and indirect referral recruitment.

149. Viral loop their social post

Get the audience engaged in the social media content you have created by enticing them to share, and get others they know to share as well. The idea behind viral loops is to tap into several degrees of sharing among your target audience, especially those you cannot reach directly. This can be achieved by creating an incentive to share, such as giving away a prize, and every time they share this opportunity with someone else they can get another chance to enter. This increases their possibilities of winning. Make this prize worthwhile and do this frequently.

150. Export posts on trending topics

Invite top growth hackers to give their opinions on trending topics in the growth space. Using their opinions and inputs in an optimized format, popularize this as a media post under your brand. Push engagement to show interest for those participating. The secret behind this is to tap into top talent in a light and low friction way, showing your support for talent development. At the same time, this gives you an opportunity to build rapport and target key recruits.

151. Dedicated hiring page

Aside from the article and the social posts, you need a dedicated growth hacking page to house all that content. This way, you can post jobs, success stories and more, to help brand your company towards growth hackers.

152. Feature top performers

Use your dedicated growth hacking hiring page to celebrate your top performers. This is a great way to celebrate your own talent internally, but also to attract new ones. Use this opportunity for storytelling. Using a format that includes where they started, how they became part of your organization and what they aspire to do next. The secret behind storytelling is making the top performers more relatable to those who you want to hire next. This lowers the barrier of entry but also increases the interest levels.

153. Featured growth hacks

Utilize your dedicated growth hacking hiring page to spotlight the success of growth hacks implemented. This shows the type of standards, creativity and aspirational ideas your organization is seeking and helps to develop. The secret behind this is that it can be used as part of your interview process as case-interviews. This allows those who are interested to follow and learn and eventually develop their own skills externally before applying to your organization.

154. Always have openings

Capitalize on your dedicated growth hacking hiring page to continuously capture talent. If you do not have an active vacancy, do not stop applications from coming in. Be very straightforward in your communications to manage expectations. This doesn't mean leaving openings without action but rather the challenge of filtering, and continuing to have a relationship with those potential hires until a position becomes open. That pre-recruitment retention is a challenge, and integrating your content development to attract new talent would best be applied in this case.

155. Vibing the place - shadow day placements

Tap into your dedicated growth hacking hiring page to have shadow days on which you allow potential hires to come and shadow. Shadow days are opportunities for a future potential recruit to spend a day working alongside one of your full-time growth hackers. This can be done physically, ideally, but also virtually. It would make sense to have a 1:3 or even 1:4 ratio, so that you can have 3-4 people shadowing a single person. The secret behind this is to filter and see who would be a fit based on the interest of the potential recruits, knowing what is expected. Having this on your dedicated page allows you to recruit, and put videos of past shadow day participants.

156. Open coffees days

Promote your open coffee days on your dedicated growth hacking hiring page. The key behind an open coffee day is to have your top decision makers present, including your head of growth. This not only attracts the interest of future recruits, but also presents an opportunity for questions and answers to determine interest and fit. The secret behind this is ultimately an informal setting not a recruitment interview. This paves the way to finding a potential fit and moving them to a formal interview process.

157. Internship opportunities

Use your dedicated hiring page for growth hackers to post current and upcoming internship placements. It would be a good idea to gamify the process so you can tap into the interns' network by getting more interns into the program. Keep this consistent and use video testimonials from past internship placements on your dedicated hiring page. The secret behind this is to keep this ongoing all the time to keep the inflow of potential recruits coming in. At the same time, tap into the interns' network to unlock hidden talent you would normally not find or be able to reach.

158. Events and conference announcements

Use your dedicated landing page as a place to promote and get sign-ups for events and conferences you run. It is a good idea to have small yet frequent internal events to keep the community awareness up. The secret behind this is to get engagement, build your own access points to the growth hacking community and drive awareness both in the short and long term. This also gives you direct access to talent and can be used as a recruitment channel, both for direct recruits and indirect referrals.

159. Drop the bait in groups

Go to the growth hacker groups and drop in results, such as how many comments, or highlight a specific comment you liked. This stimulates competition and lets the best arise, seeing other channels are outperforming their own communities. The point is to get engaged and draw them into your recruitment strategy.

160. Say "no" and challenge

Find a popular comment, and outright disagree – loudly, but politely and diplomatically. Draw others into the dialogue, and then ask challenging questions to get them to put their opinions forward. More importantly, ask for facts, such as experiences they have actually had. The secret behind this is to challenge the best thinkers and bring them out of hiding. Use this as a way to find, qualify and engage potential recruits.

161. Value bomb, leave it out

Create a massive amount of value instantly, but don't give the end or final result. Leave them hanging. The secret behind this is to create curiosity and get engagement by leaving the audience asking for more. The idea is to create visibility for your hiring brand, get them interested and eventually directly recruit those who engage positively.

162. Tell a story they can associate with and leave the end out

Tell a story with a common frustration, using NLP (Neurolinguistic programming) techniques to stimulate the audience. Leave a dilemma at the end with a request for help from ad guidance. The secret behind this is being able to attract interest with the story and association but also to engage in getting help. This helps you to see who is willing to be helpful, give value and engage. Those can be very valuable recruits.

163. Turn communities on each other - but keep it nice

Take something proving from another community and cite the source. Create a debate in the community and bring others from different communities into the dialog. The secret behind this is getting hidden talent to share their ideas, resources and techniques. This allows you to see them in action and short-list potential recruits.

164. Become an admin

Communities suffer from not having enough resources to support their ongoing engagement and growth. Become an admin to help out and use that opportunity to drive more visibility. The secret behind this is showing and driving leadership in the community itself, and using direct connections outside public visibility to recruit.

165. Growth training and academies

Growth academies and online courses are great places to find emerging talent. These are usually entry level talent but they possess a lot of potential. Finding them early can prove to be very fruitful.

166. Ask the trainer

Head over to the top course websites and find those who run growth hacking courses. Reach out and let them find you the best students they've got. Here are some places to start:

- Growth Ninja School
- Reforge – Growth Series
- Growth Tribe
- GrowthHackers – Full Beginners' Course
- CXL – Growth Marketing Mini Degree
- Ultimate Beginners Course to Growth Hacking 101
- Skillshare – Basics of Growth Marketing
- Foundr.com
- Growth Hacker Marketing Course
- GrowHack
- OneMonth
- GrowthHackingCourse.io
- Gimme Growth
- Udemy – Funnel Optimization
- Udemy – GH for Startups
- GrowthX Academy

167. Ask the trainer for direct recruitments

Simply ask the trainer to refer to your organization's current and active students who they see as great hires. The secret behind this is to get them to filter and recommend. Don't forget to compensate the trainer for their efforts.

168. Ask the trainer for past student recruitments

Simply ask for past students who they have not been actively working with or thinking about. This triggers them to go back and filter the top students they have seen and refer them. The secret here is to provide a healthy referral fee for their efforts.

169. Ask the trainer to mention recruitment in their courses

Beyond active recruitment, ask trainers to mention recruitment opportunities in their content, community or even in the course itself. This also can be done in the form of an email campaign but ensure this is done on a regular basis. The secret behind this is the passive flow of recruitment referrals, with very little effort, based on effective messaging in the right places connected to good course content.

170. Ask the trainer to host a community recruitment event

Have the trainer run a 45-minute event online after their cohort of students finish, for recruitment purposes. The secret is to organize all of it for them so that all they need to do is ensure the students show up.

171. Ask the trainer to host an event for your organization

Find the best trainers with the best reach, and ask them to host a 30-60 minute virtual event on a specific topic they are very well known for. Keep this consistent by asking them afterwards to host another event or two and repeat this across at least 10-12 trainers a year. The secret behind this is that it gives you a volume of content, at events and engagement opportunities, tapping into the trainer's network and attracting new growth hackers as potential recruits.

172. Recruit the instructor

If the students are not working out for you, hire the instructor! This might open their network for other top trainers who might be for hire. Do not be shy to compensate them for their efforts.

173. Top 10 instructor list

Issue a periodic top instructor list for growth hacking courses and training. Break this down into categories, ideally 10-12. Aim to have 10 instructors per category, giving you a total coverage of 100 instructors you can rotate over a period of time. The secret behind this is that you will have a very well-structured hit list for recruitment. It also serves as a way to create credibility around your own growth hacking hiring practices, but most importantly is engaging the instructors.

174. Give instructors' awards

Leveraging a top 10 instructor list and its categories, use this as an award-giving mechanism. This enables you to highlight key target instructors you want to hire or bring in recruit referrals. The secret behind this is doing this consistently and periodically. At the same time, strategically target instructors you want to hire or those who can give a good flow of recruitment referrals. The important part is to be direct and have a support structure, especially if you're going to be sourcing recruitment referrals via the instructors.

175. Feature list of courses and instructors

Develop a list of approved courses run by top instructors. Be very specific about what courses or programs are of interest to your recruitment. Explicitly list those parts of those courses that are important to your recruitment process. Set up a cross-referral program with the instructors or the academy running the course. The secret behind this is that you are giving them credibility by approving their courses; at the same time, it's a way to recruit. Periodically updating this feature and approval list keeps the instructor on their feet and engaged with your recruitment process.

176. Request a model at the end of their course for recruitment

Find instructors to strategically sign with and request a recruitment module to be added to their course. The key here is having a structured process for this. This would include topics such as how to take the skills learned and apply them to the real world. Then, convert that into direct employment opportunities. It would also be wise to include what employers are looking for and how to best prepare. The secret behind this is helping course creators and instructors better monetize their courses, by giving the instructor a way to hook the students and monetize their skills at the end of the course itself.

177. Offer a co-branded recruitment offering

In addition to having a recruitment module added to a course, have a direct recruitment referral program inside the course itself. This would be a massive incentive at the end of the course if students can use their investment in the course to find a growth hacking job. The secret behind this would be having an easy but effective assessment at the end of the course that leads into direct recruitment. This would also compensate the course creators and instructors as a new revenue stream.

178. Host an instructor event

Round up all the key and top instructors and have an exclusive event on growth hacking training and its future. This is a good way to attract new instructors in the field and to learn the latest developments as well. The secret behind this is to add the agenda of what your organization needs and get instructors to talk about the importance of those requirements. This would have to be engineered in an engaging way to add value to the instructor and the audience. At the same time, this is a great way to draw in future students. This is great for new entrants but also advancements for more experienced practitioners in the growth hacking space.

179. Recruit the instructor's team

The instructor will have a team. If you have found them, approach them directly or do the same as getting referrals. Remember to compensate them for their efforts.

180. Get them all on LinkedIn

LinkedIn is powerful, so use it to find all the instructors and start with a connection. With some simple and easy-to-use bots you can like all posts and shares, including lightweight neutral comments. This way, you set the stage by giving support. Find ten strong, longer posts, then comment, like and share one of them. This shows a real interest and they will catch it in their notifications and analytics. Then, make a post about your growth hacking activities and mention them; this will nudge them to comment and get them engaging. The secret here is that once you have them engaging back, this is the time to strike with a direct message suggesting either a direct recruitment or a recruitment referral.

181. Introduce instructors to growth mentors

Be the one to connect. Being central and adding value in your network puts you in a powerful position. Bringing the right people together within the same space adds a lot of value. The secret to this is about showing value, leveraging your existing network and reaching out to both and directly recruiting or working on generating recruitment referrals.

182. Invite instructors to your own course building

Start your own growth hacking courses, and have them cover a very specific part. Invite the instructors and say they have been shortlisted among several top leaders in the space. Engage them in content development to see their talent in action. This serves a few goals; first, collaborations with key credible people in the space, using that content to attract other talent within the space and finally, the opportunity to recruit that instructor.

183. Tap into instructors for an open coffee day

Get the instructors to give a 15-minute talk to your top decision-makers on an open coffee day. The secret is to engage the instructor in your own space. This allows you to see the instructor in action, covering something related to your own challenges as well.

184. Feature an instructor in your newsletter

Approach one of the instructors, and ask them to be featured in one of your email newsletters on a specific topic. The secret to this is to engage them in your own challenges and see their thoughts on it, at the same time giving them space to shine. This enables you to build rapport, and use this as an entry conversation to direct recruitment or recruitment referrals.

185. Remix the instructors

Get more than one instructor from competing courses and invite them to an event, interview or article. The idea here is to get counter opinions and show your ability to draw in top talent within the growth hacking space. The secret to this is using your pulling power to bring attention to your brand and get instructors showing an interest in your business. By doing so, this enables you to have deeper technical off-side conversations with the different instructors. This will allow you to directly recruit them or source indirect recruitment referrals.

186. Build an instructor directory

On your dedicated growth hacking hiring page, have a directory of instructors you recognize across the industry. This allows you to demonstrate your ability to reach inside the industry and gain access to the top talent. The secret behind this is to rotate this directory, by updating it quarterly, and reach out to the instructors for updates. This can be new data points you create or even just what's new on their end to be added to the directory. This is a great way to keep instructors passively engaged with your hiring process to generate indirect recruitment leads.

187. Join yourself

Join the course, and learn; get to know the instructor, and his or her team. Then, find a way to interact with students, which is a great breeding ground for seeing talent at work.

188. Recruit the students

Join the course, and get to know the students. Some will be directly visible in your course, though some will be less visible; they may be in a support community or other places. The point is to find both groups of students. The secret is to identify them and build a relationship with them. Get their opinions on the course content and even some of the results they have managed to gain from the course itself. Build your recruitment hit list from there and recruit them.

189. Get students to recruit

As part of the process of tapping into the students who are part of the course, identify those who are open to being directly recruited. Ask them questions as you get to know them, such as whether they are currently working for a company or doing client work; how much of the course they have implemented and what results they have achieved. These are gateway questions to identifying recruits.

190. Hire the instructor(s)

This is very simple: get to know the instructor, build rapport and see if the instructor can be hired. Remember, this doesn't have to be a full-time position; it can be advisory, consulting or even a part-time job. This might be the most ideal way to tap into such talent.

191. Tap into the instructor's network

Follow your instructor on social media and especially LinkedIn, and identify talent via their network. You can leverage the instructor for a warmed-up introduction that may help with the recruitment process.

192. Tap into reviews, comments and testimonials

Go to the reviews, comments and even testimonials for the course and the instructor and connect with them. From there, get their inputs into the course itself and real outcomes they have managed to benefit from. They may be bought in and not willing to tell much, in which case you will have to craft a clever way to get real feedback. The secret behind this is to get to know them and see if they can be directly recruited or even refer potential recruits.

193. Find their community support

Join the support community and be active. See the top talent at work, and use this as a covert approach to hiring top talent. Do not advertise your presence for recruitment purposes.

194. Present new cases within their support community

Need a solution to a new growth problem, or even a new perspective on an old one? Tap into their support community. The secret behind this is to find not only active members to emerge and see their thoughts and ideas, but also to identify passive members by challenging them to see what you're up to. The secret behind this is firstly to be active and seen as an active member; and secondly, it gives you an opportunity to see talent in action and target them for future recruitment. To gain direct contact, create an online form to collect different ideas, and when they emerge within the support community ask them to fill out the form as a way to capture their ideas; this will help you to get their direct contact.

195. Share new data within their support community

Got something interesting to share? Put it directly into the support community and ask for their thoughts on this new data. Encourage them to come up with challenging ideas or even provoking perspectives. The secret behind this is to gain insights from the support community itself, but at the same time to see emerging talent within the support community and recruit them directly or for recruitment referrals.

196. Share award-giving within their support community

Advertise an award being given away. Post the award-winners within the support community and share their story. The story will inspire others to apply in the future but show your active participation in the support community and in the overall growth hacking space.

197. Share new growth hacks within their support community

No great growth community is complete without sharing the actual growth hacks themselves. Don't just share ideas; share outcomes and results too. Ideally, include data and numbers the support community can sink their teeth into. This enables further engagement by getting more ideas or validations etc. The secret here is engagement, attention, and more importantly to gain access to the top talent within that support community.

198. Share events and conferences within their support community

Get your calendar on to the support community, whether that be your own events and conferences or others you're participating in. Don't just announce your participation and channel that participation through your organization. For example, if it's an external event, you may want to sponsor four entities, fully paid, and put that into the support community as a way to support the community itself. The secret behind this is giving value, but also gaining access to those who want to develop more and be active. You will be able to see their talent in action. This is a more passive approach but its biggest benefit is building rapport for direct recruitment or for recruitment referrals.

199. Share open coffee day invites within their support community

Use your open coffee day to invite members of the support community to participate. Always position it as limited seating within a set deadline. This urgency forces those who are most interested to participate. At the same time, it notifies them that your top decision-makers will be present, gives them a hook to be there and even an opportunity to participate by asking questions or offering insights. The secret behind this is engaging future recruits on a softer basis to get to know them and show that your organization is interested in top growth hacking talent.

200. Consistently answer questions within their support community

Be an active member. Don't let a good question or comment pass without at least a minimal response. This gives you visibility for existing members but also helps you capture newly added members

Let's hire the best talent

This exercise helps identify the best hacks to hire talent. This enables you to track performance, re-use top performers, discard poor performers, and create new hacks that might outperform existing ones. Choose hacks you want to use. Write down the number and name of the hack. Once a hack is applied, capture top-level learning points and the result.

Hack | # | Name of hacked
Learning | | What did you learn?
Result | | What are the results?

Hack | # | Name of hacked
Learning | | What did you learn?
Result | | What are the results?

Hack | # | Name of hacked
Learning | | What did you learn?
Result | | What are the results?

Hack | # | Name of hacked
Learning | | What did you learn?
Result | | What are the results?

Hack | # | Name of hacked
Learning | | What did you learn?
Result | | What are the results?

Performance of hacks

Capture, top, and poor performance hiring hacks here. At the same time, generate new hacks by combing existing hiring hacks or using existing hacks to inspire a new hiring hack. Use this performance page to develop your next action plan with your team to outperform your competition in finding, attracting, and retaining top growth talent.

Top performing Hacks

Hack   #   Name of hacked

Hack   #   Name of hacked

Hack   #   Name of hacked

Poor performing Hacks

Hack   #   Name of hacked

Hack   #   Name of hacked

Hack   #   Name of hacked

New Combo Hacks

Hack   #   Name of hacked   #   Name of hacked

Hack   #   Name of hacked   #   Name of hacked

Hack   #   Name of hacked   #   Name of hacked

New generated hacks

Hack   #   Name of hacked

Hack   #   Name of hacked

Hack   #   Name of hacked

in the support community. Always connect new answers or comments to other resources you have, such as a landing page with more information, or a previously answered question in the same support community. This reinforces your ability to influence members of the support community.

201. Cross-share content from one support community to the other

If you're a member of several support communities, do not waste content and efforts; reuse them in other support communities. Do this wisely by ensuring there are not duplicates, in case members below join other support communities. This helps your organization optimize the time, efforts and costs spent in support communities.

202. Join their mastermind

Some of the support communities have extended support tools such as a mastermind group (group of peers who meet to give each other advice and support). Join it and find the top talent from within. This might be a good breeding ground for your growth team to also join to help find talent but also to help solve internal growth challenges.

203. Provide specific content to their mastermind

Every mastermind operates differently, with different rules. Decide on a focus area in growth and growth hacking and keep it consistent. Of course, this must be within context and relevance to the mastermind. The secret behind this is to access your mastermind members' networks by remaining consistent on the topic, while adding value and being clear that your goal is to recruit.

204. Host their mastermind at your office or hacker house

Add more value by offering to host their mastermind at your office or hacker house, if you have one. The goal is about being top-of-mind and adding value. Being consistent helps your goals, as adding value and hosting gives you an advantage in the master-mind program. The secret to this is tapping into the network of those members in the mastermind.

205. Rotate your representation in the mastermind

Rules may differ by mastermind group but find those that allow you to rotate your representation. This allows you to place more mem-bers of your growth year within the mastermind. The secret is cov-ering more ground or force, but a change of voice with the same message gives the goal even more emphasis.

206. Bring your strategic resources to the mastermind

Bring new data, tools, networks, ideas and anything else you can get validation for, support with or even collaboration on. The point is that when you bring them from a growth perspective you tie in the remaining members into your growth goals by coming with value. The secret here is being up-front and adding value; this empha-sizes the need for some slight pressure on other members to help you achieve your goal of recruiting the best growth hackers.

207. Bring new challenges into the mastermind

Tackling a new growth program? Bring it to the mastermind and tap into new resources and ideas. The secret here is not only to posi-tion yourself for access to support directly and within their network but also to position the need to always recruit the best possible tal-ent.

208. Invite an award-winner to a mastermind

Tap into your network of award-winners – if you run such a campaign, of course. Leverage them as new forms of talent you promote externally to bring a new perspective to the mastermind. The secret behind this is warming up the talent you want to hire by showing them your value to them, and showing the caliber of talent you want to hire to other mastermind members to get them to help recruit for you.

209. Massage the ego

Reconditions go a long way. They genuinely are a great way of demonstrating good faith with others. This also assists you because if others are not arranging them and you are, this gives you a competitive advantage in hiring.

210. Give an award

Create your own industry growth hacking specific award. Make it periodical in nature, and have several categories so that you can award more than one growth hacker in one cohort of awards. PR this and get it out there, and drive the story behind those growth hackers so that those admiring their hard work may be your next hires.

211. Segmented awards for growth hacking

Giving a single award is one thing, having several well-segmented awards can be powerful. For example, you could include segments such as top B2B growth hacks, top SaaS growth hacks, top Startup growth hacks, top media industry growth hacks etc. The secret behind this is having at least 10-12 segments without having overlapping winners. This also helps you to identify talent within key segments that matter to you. When tackling indirect segments, you will find crossover talent and that may be where you find your best growth hacking talent.

212. Ranking systems to give growth hacking awards

Having a ranked order system whereby there is a single winner but multiple runners-up can be very powerful. This encourages new talent or rising talent to do better but also shows what people need to do to be recognized within your campaign. This can work very well with segmented awards in the growth hacking space; for example, top B2B growth hacks, and having the top 10 ranks, with the first being the winner, of course. The secret behind this is to unlock more hidden talent in the growth hacking space and attract them to your organization.

213. Have a dedicated YouTube playlist for your awards

Do not let your efforts get diluted in other marketing and public relations efforts. Have a dedicated YouTube playlist, on which you announce and do interviews with the winners or those who are runner-ups. The secret behind this is creating content that has a longer shelf life than the announcement itself. This way, it can be search engine optimized and with a call to action to nominate yourself or someone else for the next round, giving this a long-term yield.

214. Go live on social with the awards giveaways

Alongside creating content around your winners, go live with them on social media. The screen behind would be to tap into their networks. Don't be shy in using LinkedIn Live, which is one of the top fetching engines when it comes to cracking candidates' professional networks rather than their social network. List it as an event, and have participants register in advance. That database allows you to re-market to the same network with future events and to bring them into your recruitment funnel later on.

215. Have a dedicated section within your hiring page

Do not forget to have a dedicated section within your growth hacking hiring page. This is a great way to demonstrate your ability to reach beyond your own employees and show recognition for top talent. This is a clear indicator that you are an employer who has played growth hacking and is active in the development of your own talent.

216. Feature award-winners in email newsletters and signatures

It is important to use your own existing assets, such as an email newsletter and an email signature. Announce your winners in a dedicated newsletter and use small features to tell their stories over time. At the same time, use your email signature across the organization to celebrate those winners to attract more talent via your own network.

217. Combine awards with an event or conference

Find an important external event or conference and partner with them, for the award giveaways. This is a nice way to soften the agenda as a larger event for something more meaningful. This way, you can use the spotlight of attention at the event or conference to further drive your awards program.

218. Give recognition

Beyond an award, create specific recognitions, such as top community support, or social sustainability, top female growth hackers etc. Softer, more impactful subjects are powerful. Use this as an ad hoc form of recognition, beyond the awards system you have already set up.

219. Promote that recognition on social media

Connect with those to whom you have given recognition and promote them via social media. Build a story around them to get others inspired. The secret here is to build a rapport with the growth hacker you have recognized, and then either recruit directly or ask for a recruitment referral. Additionally, this helps your brand to attract other growth hackers, who will see those with talent being recognized and appreciated.

220. Give recognition frequently

Turn your recognition into an ongoing practice. For this hack to work, it cannot be sporadic but rather a frequent and regular event that others can predict, in order to build anticipation. It would be a wise idea to brand this activity and build a dedicated landing page or use your hiring landing page to keep all of your recognitions visible in one place. The minimum frequency would be monthly and the ideal would be weekly. The secret behind this is that the frequency makes hits predictable and opening this up to external nominations will widen your network even further into other areas to identify hidden growth hacking talent.

221. Get those you've recognized to form a community

Once you hit a minimum target inventory of recognitions, 25 for example, start engaging them into a community. This enables more frequent, direct engagement with them but, more importantly, it encourages them to open up their networks for indirect recruitments. The secret behind this is leveraging their networks and consistency. The combination of both will help find hidden talent within their networks.

222. Get those you've recognized to attend an open coffee day

Go beyond the recognition and get them involved in your own activities. The best starting point is giving them a 15-minute slot at an open coffee day, whether that be virtual or physical. The secret here is that when you bring together your top decision-makers and those who have been externally recognized, this creates an environment in which others want to participate to be part of this type of culture.

223. Get those you've recognized to attend your events

Got an event coming up? Tap into those growth hackers whom you have recognized. This is a great source of content development and credibility for your brand. The secret here is going beyond the recognition and giving them the power to flex their expertise. This allows you to get a deeper understanding of their talent and an opportunity to attract them into your organization.

224. Give a prize to those who have been recognized

Gamify the experience and give those whom you recognize a prize. This goes beyond the recognition itself and shows value. The secret behind this is showing them and others in their network how important growth hacking talent is to your organization.

225. Give a mention

Use your social media network to mention the awards and recognitions. Beyond this, use this as a way to get more micro. When you see an outstanding growth hack, mention it, even if you don't know who the growth hacker behind it is. This helps you attract those you cannot see behind the walls.

226. Give a mention and ask a question

Utilize your social media networks by mentioning an award or a recognition for the growth hacker. Engage that growth hacker by asking an insightful question to get them engaged and to get the audience interested in what they have to say. The secret behind this is being able to build rapport, massage their ego and then communicate directly with them about recruitment or recruitment referrals.

227. Give a mention and ask for their story

If you're tapping into social media to mention an award or a recognition for the growth hacker, go a bit deeper to massage the ego, and ask for their story. This is a great way to inspire others within your network but also to boost that growth hacker. The secret behind this is to share positive feedback from others with the growth hacker to build quick rapport. The secret behind this is positioning those positive praises as the ideal traits of someone on your own growth team.

228. Give a mention and tag other key growth hackers

Make use of social media and mention an award or a recognition for the growth hacker. When doing so, identify 305 key external growth hackers who would be of interest to you in the future. Mention them to draw their attention and encourage them to also engage. The secret behind this is to use the recognition as a hook for other growth hackers to want the same. From there, build rapport with the growth hacks mentioned and then work directly to recruit or get recruitment referrals.

229. Give a mention and invite to your open coffee day

Take advantage of your social media and mention an award or a recognition for the growth hacker. Invite the growth hacker as a part of your open coffee day, whether that be physical or virtual. The secret here is to inform them that your top-decision makers will be present, as well as key influencers. Give them a special post to speak for 15 minutes. Once they know they are being recognized and are in front of the top decision makers, they will be more willing to make a greater impression. Once that has been achieved, reach out and state what a great impression they have made and either directly recruit them or ask for recruitment referrals.

230. Give a mention and invite to your hacker house

Make use of your social media networks to mention an award or a recognition for the growth hacker. Invite them to your hacker house; if you don't have one, create or sponsor one. This gives you an opportunity to have that growth hacker interact with your own team and evaluate whether this person would be a good fit on the growth team. The secret behind this is to build rapport, create interest and then recruit them on to the team if they fit; if they don't, ask for a recruitment referral.

231. Give a mention and invite to an external virtual event

Use your social media platforms and mention an award or a recognition for the growth hacker. If you're participating as part of an external conference or event, bring them with you. Highlight them as your top choice and use this as a direct recruitment method. The secret is that you're investing in them and trusting them by giving them the spotlight.

232. Give a mention and invite to an internal virtual event

Utilizing your social media networks, mention an award or a recognition for the growth hacker. Bring them to an internal virtual event and host them for a 15-30 minute talk to get your growth team to see whether they are a good fit. The secret here is to show that you trust them enough to host them and want to get your team to earn from them.

233. Give a special email

Track down the growth hackers behind admirable growth hacks and just give them a special ego boost. Praise their work and ask to learn from them, but mention nothing of recruitment. This enables you to test their talent, get to know their personality and eventually proposition them into a position at your firm,

234. Send a special email and invite them to an open coffee day

Massage the ego by sending a highly complimentary email about a growth hack they have done or been part of. Take this opportunity to invite them to your open coffee day, whether a physical or virtual one, and have them give a short talk on their experience. The secret here is to let them know your top decision makers will be present, and a good audience will be listening.

235. Send a special email asking for more insights

Knead the self-image by sending an exceptionally complimentary email about a growth hack they have done well. Engage the growth hacker in giving deeper insights. This continues to boost their ego. The secret here is to build rapport with the growth hacker to open the doors for direct recruitment or to request a referral to another growth hacker,

236. Send a special email inviting them to an event

Raise their self-image by sending an ego-raising email about a growth hack they have done or been essential in developing. Use your position in events or conferences you're hosting or participating in wisely. Place some of the top thinkers there and promote them. This gives you the ability to build a rapport and pave the way to accelerated direct recruitment.

237. Send a special email offering a lead role in a growth hacking course

Praise a well-known growth hacker by sending an ego-boosting email about a growth hack they have done very well. Invite the growth hacker to take on a small part of a growth hacking course. Ideally, it would be nice to have them do more, but their time will be limited. This gives you the ability to tap deeper into their skill sets and expertise. The secret behind this is building up a database of external growth hacks as cases in your content or course building and have them be part of that process.

238. Send a special email to direct recruit

Send an ego-boosting email to a growth hacker about a growth hack they have executed very well. If you see a potent opportunity for direct recruitment, go for it. Praising their growth hack, boosting their ego and asking for more insights helps to build quick rapport. Then use that to recruit them outright. This is a more direct approach which needs to be managed in a sensitive manner due to confidentiality and other related issues.

239. Send a special email to ask for a referral

Send an ego-lifting email to a growth hacker about a growth hack they have executed well. This opportunity to build rapport might provide a potent opportunity to ask for a referral to another great growth hacker. This is also a direct approach but tapping into their network. This may feel awkward, so it might be a wise idea to attempt to recruit them directly, knowing it may not work, and then introduce the idea of a referral.

240. Growth agencies are a beehive of talent

Growth hacking agencies are an excellent place to find talent. Keep in mind, 86% of them do not grow themselves. You can learn more via the growth hacking service buyer report. That said, they struggle with talent too. They are more likely to find better talent than you as their incentives are much greater.

241. Become a potential client

Give growth agencies a test drive. Approach them for a proposal, inviting their best work. In the process, ask plenty of questions, as they will be serving you. Get their names, find them on LinkedIn and other sources and start the recruitment process.

242. Bidding process to find the best growth agency talent

Invite the growth agencies to a bidding process with other growth agencies. This way, you can tackle a group of growth agencies in one shot. By doing so, and with the growth agencies being aware of the competition, they are more likely to put their best foot forward. The secret here is to find out who the team is, behind the execution of the proposal. Asking more questions about the team exposes their names and details and this enables you to recruit them later on.

243. Become an actual client of growth agencies

Become a client of growth agencies to genuinely help with your internal growth; at the same time, use this as an opportunity to see their talent at work. Read the contract carefully to ensure there are no clauses that state you cannot recruit their team members. The secret behind this is to literally find the best talent by having them do the work for you, before hiring them internally.

244. Ask for previous client references for due diligence

During the process of engaging a growth agency for potential client work, you need to conduct client references. The secret here is to see whether those clients have recruited anyone from the growth agencies before and, if they have, you may want to re-recruit them to your organization.

245. Ask questions only their best talent can answer

During a proposal process, or via their social media or blog posts, ask deep technical questions that will require a response from their best talent.

246. Ask at events where the growth agencies are

Identify which events the growth agency will be attending and speaking at, and get ready with your top questions. The best way to approach this is to ask a good question from a strong technical perspective. This tends to get half an answer, and that is the goal. This then pushes you to ask for further information – but not at that moment, later on. The secret behind this is to get to know them one-to-one and then use that initial rapport to open the door to their experts to give you more insights.

247. Identify where the growth agency has most visibility online

Identify where the growth agency is most visible online. Use that channel to ask a very pressing but powerful question from a technical perspective. This provokes an answer from their best. However, you may not see who it really is, in which case you should ask for a follow-up question for more clarity but on a direct message basis. During that process, you can request to talk directly and identify who their top experts are.

248. Create an online event and get growth agencies' top talent to speak

Create an event online and invite the growth agency to have a speaker or two. Create an agenda that will demand the top talent within their organizations, who are best able to address the topics. Create more than one speaking placement opportunity to gain more exposure to who is working on what, internally. Have people on your team positioned to ask questions as part of the audience to further identify more experts behind the scenes.

249. Create an online event and get the growth agencies' top talent to join

Create an event online and simply invite their team. Have a paid entry fee, a good agenda, and give them free entry. This low-friction, no-obligation approach enables them to surface their best talent. Give a limited number of seats as well; this way, they will pass this opportunity on to their best talent and now you can acquire their contact information to recruit them later.

250. Follow them and identify their best

Agencies will post on social media, blogs and even traditional media articles, in which their top talent will be mentioned. Find them and recruit them.

251. General followers

As with any growth agencies, there will be general followers. Some may not be very useful and others may be fake, but there will also be those people who follow growth agencies to join them and learn from them, or they simply have an interest in the industry overall. That last segment is where you want to focus. One strategy is to use analytics to gauge levels of interest and participation, another is monitoring the likes, comments and other engagement showing active support. The secret is to identify those who are active and target them. Regarding those who are inactive, you would need to analyze carefully before targeting them.

252. Growth hacker followers

Using a simple search, you can identify whether those who follow growth agencies are growth hackers themselves, by using keywords related to growth hackers and growth hacking. This is a dead giveaway. The secret here is to target them directly. See what other activities they are engaged in, and identify others within their network you can add to your target list. Once that list is exhausted through each growth agency's account, start your targeting campaign.

253. Company followers

Not only do individuals follow, but other companies do, too. Specific growth agencies may be following supplier companies, clients, and other partners within their network without them knowing it. This serves as an opportunity to go deeper and see their networks as a source from which to identify growth hackers and target them. The secret here is there might be companies that follow the growth agencies, which may serve you as a potential source for your list of recruits as well. Exploit those networks as well. Additionally, it would be a smart idea to have your company page follow key target hires, as a way to signal your interests indirectly.

254. Mention active followers

Once you have identified active followers behind the growth agencies, engage them in content by mentioning them. Create content campaigns that are designed to engage experts in the field and get them involved in your content. In other words, create active content, not passive. The objective is to surface the best talent and engage them before targeting them for recruitment. You may also want to data enrich their contact details to find other networks on which to follow them, and eventually identify the best network to use to reach out to them. Usually, LinkedIn would be the most potent in this case.

255. Direct message recruitment and referrals

Once you have segmented and exhausted your hit list, decide whether you want to direct recruit or bring them into your referral program. Active and well identified growth hackers are best suited for direct recruitment. Passive or not easily identifiable growth hackers are best for referrals. The secret behind this is to segment between direct action, and indirect network access to find hidden talent.

256. Comment with provoking questions

Use the growth agencies' blogs, social media and other third-party platforms to initially ask provoking questions that challenge their credibility, so that they have to find the best person to answer. This is where you will drive them and track them down.

257. Ask provoking questions and make a video about them

Get others to participate and have the growth agencies' experts offer their own opinions on the matter. This way, you can get them interested in the conversation and quote them. The secret behind this is to get the best to emerge and engage them for recruitment.

258. Use competition to stimulate engagement

Use a competitor's strength to expose the growth agency's weakness and have them comment on this. This can be painful and catchy and that is the point. This will get them engaged and interested in having to defend themselves. A lack of reply will encourage their competition you mentioned to fill in and this forces a ping-pong effect. This then allows you to watch what happens and identify the experts that emerge in the conversations.

259. Take a probing question into a social media post

Take the questions elsewhere. For example, if you ask a provoking question on their blog, screenshot it and share it on their social media and comment on there to get the reply. Repeat this across other platforms. This can be seen as aggressive; therefore, you may want to use an anonymous account rather than your organizational account or personal handles. At the same time, monitor who jumps in from outside the organization and see what they bring to the table.

This will open up other potential networks and identify hidden talent to be recruited.

260. Target the public speaker

If the growth agency has one of their people speaking in public at a forum, position the provoking question online on that platform. They are more likely to reply, and then use the following conversation points to get others within their organization to emerge. Ask questions such as "How does your team deal with....?" Bring into context the team beyond the speaker.

261. Contradicting opinions of speakers

If you find two speakers at a conference or event with very different opinions, inject a provoking question to one and leverage the other. Do the same the other way. You can do this via public platforms or even their social media accounts. The idea is to be diplomatic about this, without harming anyone, but spark a fiery conversation that will allow you to see who emerges into that conversation in the midst of that battle. Those who emerge in this conversation are your targets for recruitment.

262. Question and coffee

Throw a provoking question to an expert, and invite them to an open coffee day, whether virtual or physical. This gives you an opportunity to position the conversation around your brand. This attracts the invitee, of course, but also their audience into an interesting topic or conversation. This helps you to identify the best talent for recruitment.

263. Promote a killer answer

Once you have an amazing answer or insight from an expert or someone within the audience, promote it. Use social media to gain visibility on that reply. By doing so, this helps tap into the audience of the expert who provides the killer answer. Remember, you don't have to keep this post; you can delete it in the future if it doesn't flow with your current social media strategy. Alternatively, you can take this to another platform where this might work better. The point is that you're creating a conversation to attract the top minds.

264. Call out a growth thought leader

Ask a provoking question on the source platform of the talent you are targeting and request a growth thought leader to reply. The secret behind this is that when you use their audience to get someone else to give the answer, they naturally feel left out. This then stimulates them to get their next experts to join the conversation. This enables you to identify their top talent and recruit them.

265. LinkedIn search the agency

Find their agency company page on LinkedIn, click on People and see who works there. Do not forget to check for people who have formerly worked there, too. If they have a job opening, create a ghost profile and apply so that you can see who else has applied.

266. People under agency company profile

Identify top growth agencies across LinkedIn. You may be interested in geography, and that would make sense, but it's also important to keep in mind that with virtual working formats and remote work, your scope can be much larger. On LinkedIn, once you have found an agency, follow them and within their company profile you can click on People and see everyone. This builds a direct recruitment hit list.

267. People formerly with the agency

Beyond the key agencies and the people who are actively working for the agencies, find the former employees. In the search filters, select former employees rather than current. This builds your next recruitment hit list.

268. People connected to agency employees

Beyond the obvious aim to tap into existing employees who work for the agency, the question is to see who they are connected with. This is where the real power of LinkedIn comes into play. By seeing who their key growth team members are connected to, you will see a few things emerge. First, you will learn which growth hackers are looking for a job; second, you will find other agencies you did not identify previously; and third, you may spot emerging talent not yet on the radar. Continue to build that recruitment hit list.

269. People connected to former agency employees

Identify former agency employees, and see who they are connected to. This will open up more visibility for further building your recruitment hit list on LinkedIn. The secret behind this is seeing what you didn't know exists. Networks go much deeper than what is immediately visible, and LinkedIn is perfect for this.

270. People commenting on their posts

Take your growth agency hit list, and see who's commenting on all their posts. This can take time, and there are growth hacking tools to help with this. The secret behind this is to identify who is actively working around or with the agency that you cannot see in their network directly.

271. Group siphoning

Tap into the groups the growth agency is directly part of or supporting indirectly. It would be a wise idea to find groups that their employees are part of, and former employees too. This will help identify other hidden networks of growth experts on LinkedIn.

272. Find the experts and give them a challenging question

Take your hit lists across all activities to source and build your hit list and start asking challenging questions. There are two ways to approach this. The first is direct, where your organization is visible and you ask the questions. The indirect option is to have another LinkedIn account set up, where your organization is not visible. Both have their own benefits strategically. If you don't want to be detected, use indirect; if you're ok with it, go direct.

273. Like and comment on all posts for visibility

Using your direct account on LinkedIn for visibility, you can use a passive approach and automate the process to simply like and comment on all people identified on recruitment hit lists. Comments don't have to be very rich, just simple comments that are supported naturally. The secret behind this is for them to see a pattern of interest and eventually reach back out to your firm or your recruiter directly.

274. Google My Business

Look at who has reviewed and liked and even asked questions about your business. Check if any of them are growth hackers and see if they can be recruited. Google My Business is a local business listing in Google Optimize to help those searching to find your business without your website getting in the way. This helps to optimize natively into the Google search engine.

275. Questions and answers

Utilize the question-and-answer component of Google My Business. Most people use the reviews and other features. Use the Q&A part to surface a good question to get their top growth expert to answer. This will most likely result in a front-end social media person, who will point you to further resources. Get in touch with that person and have them guide and channel you towards the growth team and help you get the names and positions of who those experts are. They often have access to a directory of some nature and that is the secret to it.

276. Leave a review as a question

Go to the reviews, and leave questions. It's so out of place that it yields attention. By doing so, you will get a reply from a front-line responder, and the secret is to get them to channel you to the right experts within the organization.

277. Give a low rating with a question to get attention

Nothing gets more attention than a low rating. Positioning a slightly conversational or challenging question with a low rating will do the job. This is destined to get their front-line responders to open their internal channels to get you to their growth team and identify who the key experts in that team are.

278. Reply to a low-rated review with a question

Take the next step: instead of being the one to give the low rating, use others' low ratings to position questions for their growth hacking team. This could be staged in progressive questions across several low-rated reviews to really get under their skin. This then forces them to reply, and you can ask for a way to channel your concerns to the growth team.

279. Analyze reviews to see if experts have emerged

Maybe someone has already done the work for you. It's highly un-likely, as this is not a common channel for such activity by another growth hacker who may be a step ahead of you. This would be a great opportunity to analyze and see if someone else is siphoning talent. Regardless, leverage this opportunity.

280. Reviews and comments

Look anywhere else besides Google My Business where comments and reviews are placed. See if there are growth hackers, track them down and see if they are top talent. If so, discover whether they can be recruited.

281. Comments with questions

Place a basic growth hacking question that only someone from the growth hacking arena can answer. The secret behind this is to iden-tify who the experts are behind the scenes. Do not be shy to re-quest a further one-to-one or direct, in-depth answer.

282. Bring in controversial answers for comments

Challenge one of the popular answers with a controversial opinion, insight, answer or even question that challenges what has already been deemed to be the right or best answer. The secret behind this is to get their best expert to emerge and become visible in the process. You can close the circle by replying with a request for direct communication.

283. Request more insights

Agree with an answer or even simply request more insights on the question itself or one of the top answers. This way, you are able to create more depth, but more importantly you can identify the expert internally. Keep in mind that through this process, others within a community or on any online platform may reply and this might also serve as a way to recruit someone who has the insights.

284. Request more resources

Beyond a good answer, request more resources based on the top answers. This will encourage more information and, by further asking beyond that, you can find the expert. The secret is to find the expert or experts behind the answers, who you can recruit.

285. Request a direct message or contact

When the opportunity is right, make a direct request to get in touch. They may initially offer a general contact point and that would be purely due to spam threats. Use the general contact point, and from there dig deeper to find who the experts behind the growth team are.

286. Use a well-known opinion and ask for their views

It's possible to stimulate direct contact from scratch by surfacing a common opinion and challenging them with a reply to that. This is best used when you don't see a direct opportunity within their reviews or comments to interject. The secret behind this is to surface their best talent and then get in touch with them directly.

287. Let's have a coffee

There's no better way to build rapport than having a coffee together. Make it an event without all the cost and headaches, but let's growth hack this.

288. Open coffee day

Have pre-scheduled coffee days at your own office where potential recruits can drop in and just network with the top brass at your firm. Use this as a way to get to know talent on a personal level; it's not an interview.

289. Limited seating to open coffee day

Keep your open coffee day with limited seating. You may start with an invite-only approach. The secret here, which is quite simple, is scarcity. Use scarcity wisely to empower your audience to want to be part of this unique event.

290. Specialist guests for open coffee day

Get someone well-known as a celebrity in the growth hacking space. An open coffee day is designed to be physical; you may have to fly them in. This will be worth it when they are able to attract a wider audience to your coffee day. This celeb may be in your area for an event or something else and you can leverage their schedule to attract them to your open coffee day.

291. Access to top decision makers on open coffee day

Ensure you have your top brass available on your coffee days. Growth hackers want to connect with the right people and the top people. This is not just a form of attraction, but also a chance for your top decision-makers to get a sense of the talent pool that is being recruited and to engage with them.

292. Giveaways to gamify open coffee day

Have a valuable giveaway to attract top talent to the open coffee day. It's very simple: use this as a hook to attract the attention required, filter it to the right audience and invite them to the open coffee day.

293. Short-form content from open coffee day

Use the opportunity to create small 60-second clips designed for YouTube shorts, Tiktok, Instagram and other social media platforms to get others interested in future open coffee days. This helps to capture some of the great ideas and moments received at the open coffee day for internal usage, but also provides marketing for the open coffee day. The secret behind this is to stimulate demand for the open coffee day.

294. Align open coffee day with special occasions

Got something special coming up this month, such as Christmas or Breast Cancer Awareness month? Use those special occasions to highlight them at your open coffee day. This keeps your open coffee day fresh, relevant and aligned. The secret behind this is being top-of-mind.

295. Growth hacking ideas on open coffee day

Use the open coffee day as a way to demonstrate new growth hacking ideas, or ways to generate new ones. This is a great engagement method to allow the best thinkers to emerge.

296. Invite from growth hacking communities to your open coffee day

Tap into growth hacking communities - ones you're in and even ones you're not - to give invitations to the open coffee day. This way, you can build awareness about your organization and the fact you're interested to directly engage and invest in recruiting the best talent. The secret here is to leverage the fact that your top decision-makers will be there as that will be the main hook to get them interested; then, drive recruitment.

297. Get a growth mentor to speak on open coffee day

Bring in a growth mentor or coach for one of the open coffee days to drive a wider audience reach. It's very simple: it's using celebrity / expertise power to attract others to attend and take an interest in the open coffee day.

298. Virtual coffee day

Arrange pre-scheduled coffee days online. Have a nice introduction with some updates on how to create context, but remember that it's not a formal interview. Top talent wants to meet decision-makers and getting your top decision-makers to invest 30 minutes of their time to attract talent is effective. And talk growth; get them into your mind-frame but without it being formal.

299. Virtual coffee with head of growth

Designate one of your weekly virtual coffee events to your head of growth. This gives the audience a chance to hear about the latest and greatest but also to build rapport with your head of growth. The secret behind this is for growth hackers who aspire to work at your firm to get to know your head of growth and directly approach them for recruitment purposes.

300. Virtual coffee with the CEO

Designate one of your weekly virtual coffee events to your CEO to get to know the growth hacking community and those interested in growth. Positioning key messages related to growth and growth challenges will trigger potential growth hackers to approach with their own ideas and resources to help. The secret here is to attract the right growth hackers, get them engaged, and get them to apply to your organization.

301. Virtual coffee for new launch

Got a new launch? It could be a new launch of anything; a new product, service, event, market entry or so on. Use your weekly virtual office events to launch or even pre-launch. The secret to this is aligning your interests and growth with your virtual coffee day, which is an informal touch point to connect with the growth community.

302. Take virtual coffee live on social

Go live with one or a few of your virtual coffee days. The idea is not to take them all live. The secret behind this is to attract audiences beyond your reach into your pipeline so they can become your own captive audience for your next virtual coffee day.

303. Align virtual coffees with events

Have your own event or conference, or participate in one; use the virtual coffee day to announce it and give a pre-event launch. This can help to connect your event with your audience but, more importantly, it helps to continue adding value to your virtual coffee events.

304. Virtual coffee at your hacker house

Got a hacker house? Use it as your broadcast point. Have your virtual coffees there; it is that simple. The secret behind this is to promote your hacker house, but also the culture around growth and the level of interest and investment your organization has made and continues to make in growth hacking practices.

305. Virtual coffee growth hack of the week

Feature a growth hack that has been achieved every month. This way, you can engage other growth hackers openly for input and feedback. This helps to build a rapport in an informal way to recruit some of the best growth hackers.

306. Virtual coffee award-winners and top performers

Got a new award, or recognition you have given away? Or even a top performer? The virtual coffee days are an excellent touch point to feature them and bring them to the virtual coffee day. Keep it growth-themed and allow for questions and answers to help new ideas and connections to emerge.

307. Giveaway Starbucks credits

Don't let them come to you; you go to them. Have a daily giveaway of Starbucks credits for growth hackers. Choose a few days in advance, select the locations and then come by. At the same time,

Let's hire the best talent

This exercise helps identify the best hacks to hire talent. This enables you to track performance, re-use top performers, discard poor performers, and create new hacks that might outperform existing ones. Choose hacks you want to use. Write down the number and name of the hack. Once a hack is applied, capture top-level learning points and the result.

Hack | # | Name of hacked
Learning | | What did you learn?
Result | | What are the results?

Hack | # | Name of hacked
Learning | | What did you learn?
Result | | What are the results?

Hack | # | Name of hacked
Learning | | What did you learn?
Result | | What are the results?

Hack | # | Name of hacked
Learning | | What did you learn?
Result | | What are the results?

Hack | # | Name of hacked
Learning | | What did you learn?
Result | | What are the results?

Performance of hacks

Capture, top, and poor performance hiring hacks here. At the same time, generate new hacks by combing existing hiring hacks or using existing hacks to inspire a new hiring hack. Use this performance page to develop your next action plan with your team to outperform your competition in finding, attracting, and retaining top growth talent.

Top performing Hacks

Hack   #   Name of hacked _____

Hack   #   Name of hacked _____

Hack   #   Name of hacked _____

Poor performing Hacks

Hack   #   Name of hacked _____

Hack   #   Name of hacked _____

Hack   #   Name of hacked _____

New Combo Hacks

Hack   #   Name of hacked _____   #   Name of hacked _____

Hack   #   Name of hacked _____   #   Name of hacked _____

Hack   #   Name of hacked _____   #   Name of hacked _____

New generated hacks

Hack   #   Name of hacked _____

Hack   #   Name of hacked _____

Hack   #   Name of hacked _____

171

your decision-makers have a chance to get to know talent and vice versa. It's an informal method, not an interview. Get to know their personalities first and then get into the other stuff. Keep this consistent.

308. Amazon credits

With a physical or virtual event, of course the presence of your top growth people and decision makers is one of the big hooks. Once that is in place, use Amazon gift card credits as a giveaway for signing up and showing up. Remember that many who are not your target audience may try to enter; in other words, non-growth hackers. In this case, you will need some filters in advance. Making this fun or gamifying it makes for a better experience.

309. Other credits and gift cards to attract others

Draw on the same idea as the Amazon credits; do this with other popular platforms such as Apple iTunes etc. The growth hack is the same play, but mixing up the rewards can attract different segments of the audience.

310. Credits towards your own products/services

Create your own credit scheme towards your own products and services. The secret behind this is to push your own product, of course, but at the same time, you can lower your cost of acquisition of goods or services provided as an incentive.

311. Credits towards partners' products/services

Align with your partners or suppliers and give credits away from their products and services. This plays to the same concept but again widens your offerings to consistently attract growth hackers and keep them stimulated within your network.

312. Credits towards your own growth hacking courses

Run an internal growth hacking course and give credits towards that. It's very simple; it's also widening your offerings within the scheme to attract growth hackers from outside your direct network on an informal basis for hiring purposes.

313. Let's make coffee together

Choose a location, or maybe even collaborate with a coffee shop, and make it an event. Make your coffee together as a form of bonding, but while networking informally as well.

314. Get the coffee sponsored

Work with a local coffee shop and get them to sponsor the whole idea. It's about everyone learning how to make coffee together. Mind you, there are many kitchen studios or even barista training centers that might also be willing to do this with you. The secret here is engagement. Getting people together means something you can all agree to like at some level and then build rapport. This is an informal opportunity for direct hires. It is about getting to know people and then determining whether they would be a good hire later on. It also makes sense to get the coffee shop to sponsor the event if you will be using their place frequently and driving traffic to them.

315. Give away mugs with recruitment messages

Get the coffee-making session going, but give away mugs. It's a bit overdone and old-school, but it works. Have very smart yet simple growth hacker recruitment messages or designs on the mug. The secret behind this is to popularize those mugs among the growth hacking community. This can go as far as merchandising those mugs for others who see them being shown on social media and want one too.

316. Announce a winner to get others excited

Choose the best coffee maker for that day and announce them. It's simple: it's about getting recognition but also promoting your drive to gain access to top growth hackers. The secret behind this is getting awareness and engagement via recognition.

317. Viral coffee

Get invited, and then share the invitation with three other growth hackers. The secret behind this is to get those who are interested and qualified to recruit others for you. This can become viral if several of them do this well enough. Of course, you will need to set limits to create urgency and then create a backlog of invitations for the next coffee event.

318. Let's get trained up

Why wait for others to train? Start your own basic growth hacking training courses to attract talent. This allows you to customize growth hacking towards your business and industry. This allows you better hands-on engagement. One tip: create several levels and offer the first one or few for free. If you want to make them all free, that would be effective as well, but charging a small amount doesn't show any less commitment. It's your call.

319. Set up your own growth hacking courses

Start from scratch and have your growth team make your own growth hacking training courses. This gets your team engaged and motivated internally but also helps them get what they want on their team. This is a low-risk, easy engagement method if recruiting new growth hackers.

320. Quora the course

Go to Quora.com and find the top questions asked about growth hacking courses. This will give you insights not just from the questions, but also from the comments and responses given. This insight will help you pave the way to create a growth hacking course that has impact for your industry specifically. Remember, this is designed to bring in new recruits to your organization.

321. Google top questions

Google growth hacking courses and see what questions Google has found to be common searches. Use those questions and develop your content around them. The key here is that Google has done your research for you; not just the questions, but also the priority order in which questions are asked. Use this as an outline to develop your own growth hacking course. The main point here is to be specific to your own organization and industry to attract future recruits.

322. Source comments from videos

Find growth hacking videos, and see what questions are being asked and comments that support or emphasize some of the points made. Analyze this and identify where you can develop a growth hacking course. Remember, it's best to focus on the parts that are missing or not done well.

323. Source comments from other courses

Analyze 3-star reviews for courses, identify what was done well, what was done less well and what was missing. Use those insights to develop a better course. Interact with those who have left reviews to get a deeper insight into their views. Remember, not everything that has already been covered well should be omitted, but doing it better is something that needs to be achieved at some point.

324. Source reviews from books

Analyze 3-star reviews for growth hacking-related books, where reviewers are more critical about the content in the book. This helps you identify gaps or weaknesses in the content that is available. By doing so, you can fill these gaps with a growth hacking course that covers what is not being done well or at all. It might be a good idea to interact with those reviewers and ask for more in-depth views, such as what they wished had been covered or done better.

325. Cover the common grounds better

Analyze existing courses and use the 80:20 rule. Cover the basics, not the advanced content. The secret here is to attract beginners, not advanced growth hackers. This will open a new source of recruits over a longer period of time. Once you have mastered this, you can apply the same technique to develop intermediary and advanced courses. However, without mastering the basics, the intermediate and advanced courses will not help your recruitment process.

326. Outsource and white-label your growth hacking courses

Don't have a team, or your team doesn't have time to run courses? No problem. Get someone else to do it for you and white-label it under your brand. Save yourself time, money and effort while achieving the same outcome.

327. Source from course sites

Remember, the secret here is not to create but to take an existing course and white-label it. This is an easy sell if the creator is ok with not having to create more content and using the existing content without any conflict.

328. Source from LinkedIn

Find thought leaders who have written articles or actual courses. They may have a LinkedIn course as well. Tap into this expertise and propose a white-labeled content opportunity that won't cost them anything, including time and money, of course. The secret here is introducing a new money-making channel to them, without having to change much.

329. Partner with growth academies

Find leading growth academies and find their top courses that align with your strategy for growth hacking. Approach the instructor or the academy itself and propose a white labeled money-making opportunity for their course content.

330. Find a growth mentor and tap into their existing content

Find growth mentors or coaches who have existing content that may not be in a source format. Provide them with some support such as how to put the course together with resources and tools. The secret behind this is supporting them to convert their content into a course and then a money-making channel for that content to be used.

331. Find growth thought leaders to ask if they have a course

In general, find thought leaders in the growth hacking space. This can include even academic resources that can be very useful. The secret here is finding those thought leaders who have content and a strong background but do not have a course yet. Offering to support their course development and proposing a money-making channel will be the secret to making this work.

332. Find community growth thought leaders

Within growth hacking communities you will find people with deep expertise in the field but who don't have any content, or a course. Offering to recruit them to develop a course and support them with the resources and tools will be appealing. What will be even more appealing is the money part of the equation. Remember, the goal is to use course content to attract new recruits so keep that central to your course development content.

333. Host top instructors and white-label

Get a top instructor who has a following and white-label with him or her. This brings credibility and community to the table, on top of the training and development.

334. Recruit instructors from Udemy/Skillshare etc.

Outright recruit instructors who are already creating courses on popular training websites. Sometimes, pursuing quality content from creators who are not popular might present a much bigger opportunity than from those who are overly popular. It would be wise to approach both segments and see what you can develop with them.

335. Recruit instructors from YouTube

Find top instructors who are providing course content or specific training directly or indirect on YouTube. Approach them with your offer to help support them with tools and resources. Of course, most importantly, it's a money-making opportunity to create courses for your organization. It would be very helpful if the potential instructors have a good following you can tap into as well.

336. Recruit instructors from LinkedIn

Find thought leaders and those who comment on growth-related content. If they have a consistent record of good ideas, comments and perspectives, they would be an ideal hire for a course creator. Approach them with your offer of support and resources as an organization and, most importantly, explain that this is a money-making opportunity.

337. Recruit instructors from Medium.com

Use platforms where thought leaders are writing. Approach them to ask if they have a course or have thought about building one. Check if they would be interested in developing one; your organization can provide the support and resources to make that happen.

338. Get instructors to refer other instructors

If you find a good instructor who is not interested, simply ask them to refer you to another instructor and, if that doesn't work, let them know you will check in with them again. This allows you to keep in touch with them over a period of time to see if they become more interested or if they have come across anyone else they might want to refer you to. Build this into a mailing list and follow up every 60-90 days in a passive approach, without it getting in their way. Highlight existing courses and instructors who have joined, in order to attract them.

339. Create new instructors

Find talent who can become instructors, support them with the right tools and resources and turn this into a money-making opportunity for them. The secret is building unique and great growth hacking training courses and attracting the top talent. Don't hesitate to be specific in terms of industry or different markets to attract more niche growth hackers.

340. Instructors from within

Recruit instructors from within your own organization. It's very simple; turn this into a money-making opportunity for them.

341. Growth hacking course as a drip-down email campaign

Want to keep it simple, engaging and low cost? Create a drip-down email campaign with daily training to get engagement on different levels. This is a quick and easy way to get started and it's low cost and low risk at the same time.

342. Gamify the drip-down

Create badges, levels and points, including other mechanics as well, as students move through the course. This could be as simply as gamifying their presence and drive to continue. However, it's a good idea to inject other gamification mechanics such as referrals into the course or for direct hires. Incentivizing those gamification mechanics can go a long way, as can announcing top ranks based on the gamification.

343. Send the drip-down viral

Share clips of core videos with their own edits so they can share it. For every share, incentivize the person sharing so they can share more, and get the next person to do the same. Share either the whole course itself, referrals for recruiting growth hackers, or valuable parts of the course, to attract others onto the course.

344. Direct referral in drip-down

Capture direct referrals for hiring growth hackers within the drip-down course. This can be as simple as having a button in all emails with a call to action "Hiring growth hackers". This is a direct hire approach; you might need to alternate or test a direct versus indirect approach. An indirect approach might include a "refer a growth hacker" call to action. Ideally, having both would be optimal but you need to test where to place each one.

345. Forward options in the drip-down

Strategically place a forward button in your emails and as part of your course. The secret behind this is using high value components of your course and allowing small bite-size parts to be forwarded, which they can directly share with others. The idea here is direct sharing, not sharing on two platforms, where more sharing can happen. The secret behind this is to allow the person who is forwarding to add a note. If they know someone who is solving a problem or facing a related challenge, they want to direct this value to them directly.

346. Inject a referral email in the drip-down

As they expect their next drip-down, make one of the emails a direct referral email. This allows you to tap into referrals with two options: either refer a growth hacker for hire, or refer more students to the course. If you refer more people to the course, you will have to have other direct hire lead generation placements in the course or emails.

347. Surprise in the drip-down

Provide a virtual event only for drip-down students. Offer a bonus piece of content worth $99 or more, to show value, get them onboard and the secret is to get them to share this event. When they share, they expand your reach; it gets more intakes and allows you to recruit later.

348. List key learnings and make them sharable

Bite-size your learning takeaways and allow people taking the course to share those single learnings with little context but enough to use the mystery and power of sharing to get others onto the drip-down growth hacking course.

349. Dedicate a landing page for your drip-down course

Simple but effective: have a landing page that houses all of your drip-down courses and other courses as well. Search engines optimize this to grab inward organic traffic as well. Get student testimonials and especially highlight the results they have achieved.

350. Put a mini-version of the drip-down course on other sites

This is a way to tap into inbound leads coming from other learning platforms. Place a mini-version of the course on Udemy, Skillshare and other such sites and push those intakes towards your next level growth hacking courses.

351. Student referrals

Using all of the above, get the students who enroll to get you more students. Compensate them and gamify the experience.

352. Student side hustle program

Build a side hustle for students to make money but in the context of a formal program. This way, they can find a way to pay off their student loans etc.

353. Dedicated student referral landing page

Be sure to have a dedicated landing page for student referrals, and enable viral loops to ensure you get students to refer you other students, whether it be one-off referrals or ongoing, via a compensated program.

354. Student to host on-campus event

Get a student or students to host a physical or virtual campus-oriented event. Sponsor it and support all the behind-the-scenes work and let them recruit and co-build topics and themes to drive the event. The secret to it is list-building, for future direct and indirect hiring purposes.

355. Shadow a growth hacker for a day and go live

Give a student an opportunity to live and work in the life of a growth hacker. Let them take it live on social media and promote your workplace. The secret behind this is to get into their network and present potential placement opportunities. This might also be great for developing an internship program as a next step.

356. 'Aspiring to become a growth hacker' videos

Get students who want to enter the field to make videos about why they are inspired to become a growth hacker. At the same time, stories from relatively new growth hackers discussing their experiences and how they have done well helps to attract new students but also referrals from them.

357. Gamify the student referral program

Build a gamification system around student referrals, such as points, badges and levels. This can also be incentivized with prizes and scalable compensation, based on the number of referrals.

358. Get your student referral program onto LinkedIn

Many new job seekers enter LinkedIn without much understanding of how to optimize the platform. In many ways, LinkedIn itself is more optimal for senior experienced talent. Therefore, students are seeking a way to optimize and tap into this platform. The secret here is to offer tips and hacks, but also get them into your student referral program so they can actually make money while they seek an entry-level job. This can lead to a direct hire, of course.

359. Set up a hacker house

A hacker house is a way of tapping into migrant and fringe talent. Offer them low-cost housing and perks such as food, entertainment, training, networking and parties.

360. Sponsor a hacker house

Find an existing hacker house, and simply sponsor it outright, or sponsor small parts of it such as daily breakfast or entertainment. This gives you instant exposure but also a way to build rapport with emerging fringe talent.

361. Sponsor their first hacker house party

Get that hacker house active. Throw a growth hacker party and promote it to bring attention to the hacker house. Be in charge of the guest list and membership to build your mailing list for tapping directly and indirectly in the future for recruits.

362. Sponsor hacker house course-building

Put the money behind a course to be developed and sponsored by your organization. Let the members pitch, organize and develop a course from the hacker house, sponsored and led by your organization. The secret to this is testing and tapping into expertise and eventually recruiting them.

363. Sponsor their rent in exchange for...

Simply make placement for sponsorship at the hacker house in exchange for something. This 'something' should be something of a challenge and value to both you and them. This could be as simple as building an advanced course on something very specific, or building an app for something very specific (that would be a small app, of course; nothing full blown). The point is to exchange value as part of your sponsorship in the hacker house.

364. Sponsor their growth hack

Source growth hacks outright from the members of the hacker house. Very simply, make this an easy process whereby they can ask the right questions to understand what your growth problem is and let them pitch. Find the best pitch to sponsor them to develop that growth hack.

365. Sponsor the food and get someone else to pay

Everyone loves to eat. Use your branding reach and power, and get a restaurant to sponsor food for a period of time by giving them exposure, of course, but also through you being the direct sponsor for that at the hacker house. A simple yet powerful hack in itself.

366. Sponsor a field trip

Want to have some fun? Take them somewhere for a day off. The secret behind this is to take them away from other distractions and have a focused time off to build rapport. This gives you an informal channel to start the recruitment process.

367. Get a software sponsor

Get a software company to sponsor the hacker house. Focus on tools that they will frequently use, or costly software they will need to build their next big thing. The secret behind this is that most software companies will offer some form of credit for a certain period of time.

368. Join a hacker house

Don't want to sponsor? Send one of your team members to join. It will be a nice break in some ways for your employee, but also a great way for him or her to find the best possible talent.

369. Set up hacker house events

Use your membership at the hacker house to set up a series of events. This way, you can build rapport with the hacker house members, but also tap into their networks.

370. Throw an in-house hackathons

If you're trying to solve a specific problem on your team, throw it to the hacker house. Let them solve the problem. The secret to this is to incentivize them and get them to involve others who are not part of the hacker house directly to expand your networking. This allows you to test out talent and find new growth hackers.

371. Build a virtual community for the hacker house

Being a member of a hacker house doesn't mean you cannot build a virtual community, using WhatsApp, Telegram or even Discord, to name a few examples. This way, you can tap into other hacker house members' networks and find future recruits.

372. Network with previous hacker house members

Identify previous members of the hacker house and bring them into your virtual community as alumni. The secret behind this is opening other networks, ones that may be overlooked and undervalued as they are seen only as former members of the hacker house.

373. Turn your membership at a hacker house into a reality show

Go live on a schedule on social media and turn your membership at the hacker house into a live reality show. Get other members involved; make it like a 'day in the life'-style reality show.

374. Build up hacker house content from within

Utilize the expertise in the hacker house and get them building content with you. This way, you can tap into new expertise. The secret here is to build content, of course, but also to tap into new talent and recruit the best growth hackers in the hacker house.

375. Develop a growth hacking course at the hacker house

Another way of tapping into the expertise of the talent at the hacker house is to develop courses. Bring in the necessary resources and support to make the process easier, such as structure, topics, approach and some form of consistency to build the courses. At the same time, put the marketing behind it and turn it into a money-making opportunity for the members of the hacker house.

376. Create your own hacker house

Don't want to sponsor or send someone? Create your own hacker house from scratch. That's right, your own. You call the shots, from recruitment in the house, to house rules. It's also a way to cultivate top talent in the field.

377. Set up a hacker house in your headquarters

Don't have a house right away? Use your headquarters. Turn a party into a hacker house. Ensure you're totally disconnected from your physical operations. This is a great opportunity to gain access to cultural and mindsets that don't exist in your organization. This allows for new and much more innovative growth hacking to take place.

378. Airbnb your hacker house

Don't have a hacker house or a place at your office? Rent an Airbnb and use it as a hacker house. The secret behind this is that it gives you a more flexible and low-cost approach. You can move your hacker house around, as well, and negotiate the best rates, if you're having longer stays, of course.

379. Franchise your hacker house

Create a good hacker house, get others involved and take on other locations. This is great for places you would not normally be in or do not have a strong presence. This is especially powerful in markets where you hire internationally such as India, Pakistan, Philippines and Vietnam etc.

380. Get sponsors to support your hacker house

Want to expand? Get others to support it. Find sponsors who have a vested interest in your hacker house; this would be suppliers, partners or others in your supply chain. You can get more creative and even go for sponsors such as beverage makers, and others who appeal to and want to target your younger, more dynamic audience.

381. Host regular events from your hacker house

Turn your hacker house into an event and party machine. Host weekly, monthly and quarterly events and parties. This helps get more people involved and, more importantly, expand your reach into your network to hire your next growth hacker.

382. Host a celebrity to live at your hacker house for a week

Get someone famous to live at your hacker house for a week, or a month, and go live. Think of it like a reality show. The secret to this is having a celebrity that is relevant and can be a well-known growth hacker in your space.

383. Dedicated landing page for your hacker house

Brand your hacker house for growth hackers and have your own dedicated landing page where people can apply and manage their experience with your hacker house.

384. Throw a party

Sponsor, create or join a party. They, too, need to find a way to unwind. So join the party yourself and get networking.

385. International growth hacker day

Find special occasions that matter to growth hackers and throw a party around them. Whether it be at your hacker house or another place, make the party happen. Identify unique occasions, such as international growth hacking day, etc.

386. Celebrate a growth milestone

Got a big milestone from a growth perspective coming up? Celebrate it by throwing a party and getting others involved. The secret is to get the interest of other growth hackers behind your story. Attract them by getting them to want to know more about how that milestone was achieved. This is more or less a conversation starter to identify potential future talent.

367. Virtual party, here we go

Get everyone into a single physical space and go virtual. Get growth hackers globally to attend your party and set a party theme. This would be best around a theme, an idea, or some topic that would attract people, but remember that it's a party, not training or a course.

368. Worldwide wave party

Throw a party that shifts time-zones. For example, it may start in GMT +1 for one hour then shift to the next location for another hour and on to the next major location. This would be virtual, of course, and a wise idea to get a DJ or someone to host and produce as you move around. Turn that wave into a global party no one can miss as the party comes to each guest's own time zone. And if you feel daring, you can cover as many time zones as possible.

369. Crash a competitor's party

Your competitors may have an event or party coming up. Replicate it online and throw your own virtual version of their exact party or event. If it's an event, turn it into a party, as people would much prefer a party, or if they have a party, be a party crasher. The secret behind this is to draw on their audience and campaign to drive traffic. Optimize it and grab that party. This gets the attention of growth hackers in your industry.

370. Let's get referrals hacked

Referrals are 25 times more profitable than acquiring a new client; that applies to talent, too. Networking is important and hacking those networks is a strategy of its own.

371. Get your existing employee to refer

A simple and old-school strategy is to get your existing employee to refer. Every time they refer, they get paid, and the more they refer, the more they get paid.

372. Internal training and resources to recruit

Provide a systematic yet simple program for employees to get trained, with resources to become recruiters as well. This must be incentivized as well, otherwise its impact might not be very strong. The secret to this is that the growth hackers you hire are not recruiters, but with some simple training and tools, they can do it passively.

373. Shadow a recruiter for a day

Incentivize and allow growth hackers to shadow your recruitment team. This allows both parties to benefit and learn from each other. Of course, when the growth hacker has incentives to recruit others, this will be a fruitful engagement. Although this might initially be seen as an annoyance that takes them away from their focus, you need to find a creative way to make this happen internally. Do not distract their flow, but rather find an optimal way to get this into your program.

374. A party credit

Get growth hackers who are going to their own private event or party. Give a $100-500 credit for them to go and recruit. It's like paying them to party. The secret is to remind them they should be alert for new hires, get them actively networking and help you reach dark, hidden corners within their own networks for your benefit.

375. Asking for help

When a growth hacker is networking on a professional basis with someone else in their network for help, incentivize them to use this opportunity to recruit them. For example, a growth hacker might be seeking some coding help or seeking a tool to connect to another tool and reaches out to a friend who does this well. Allow your growth hacker to give an Amazon shopping credit or a Starbucks gift card for the help, sponsored by you. Capture their information in your CRM and later remind that growth hacker internally that this person would be a good hire in the future.

376. Top-performing hires get paid more

If your current employee makes an amazing hire, pay them a bonus with their hires performance. That's the right incentive for their great referral over time. This motivates them to want to bring more top talent and to continuously search for you.

377. Scaling the performance system

Get an employee paid one for one top-performer; make a scaling compensation system. This motivates them to get more of these top-performing hires. Every time they do this and they perform well, they get an even higher pay. The secret is twofold: one is simply them making more money, but also cultivating a better team dynamic internally where they are invested in each other's performance.

378. Build an underperformance booster

If an employee recruits someone who isn't performing well, and they can help them, give them another form of compensation to get them performing better. This can be a significantly lower payout but it incentivizes teamwork and enables a strong culture of support. No one is more invested in the new recruit than the employee who brought him or her in.

379. Ranking top-recruiting employees based on top performers

Rank your top ten employees per month based on who has recruited the best performers. Of course, this would be aside from ranking your top ten performers anyway. This gives a measure internally to show who is bringing in talent as well.

380. Link top-performing recruited employee to time off

Set up a new benefit so that when a top performer performs well, those who brought them in benefit too. One of the best benefits is time off. Although they may use that time to work, it still shows good faith.

381. Recruitment, top performer linked benefits

Aside from time off, link other benefits that can be earned via the top performers recruited with the benefit to the employee who has been recruited. The secret to this is that when the top performers see others benefit from their performance, it inspires them to go and get the best talent as well.

382. Give a hiring bonus to new recruits for referrals

Got a new recruit? Give them a bonus outright at the start to get you more top hires. It's simple: get them to find clones of themselves and when they do that before starting, or even when they have just started, it gives them a boost by incentivizing them to recruit.

383. Get another firm's new recruit

Go to new hires in new competing organizations, and get them to hire for you without hiring them, so there is no conflict.

384. Announce hiring bonus on job sites

Post on job sites that you have just made a massive undisclosed payout for a new recruit to bring in another new recruit.

385. Social media post on bonus payout

Don't reveal how much it is or who has had a massive payout for a new recruit. Announce it, but don't give details. It has to be a bit mysterious and even blurring out a six figure number that is deemed representative can get people very stimulated to recruit for you or apply directly.

386. Get the new recruit to share

Get your new recruit to announce and share via social media that they just brought in another recruit with the theme and just got a generous payout. The secret is to prepare all post content for them so that they can simply adjust and post it.

387. Reality show announcement

Got a reality show, or planning to make one? Use the reach of this platform and announce that new recruit payout. Always remind the audience that this is a new recruit who has brought a new recruit with them.

388. Starbucks gift cards for one year for both recruits

As a bonus, give a year's worth of Starbucks gift cards. The secret to this is to invite other future potential recruits to coffee and introduce them to your organization. Make it easy and low friction; when incentivized, it's a smooth system in the making.

389. Open referral payments

Someone random has an ability to get your talent. Let them get paid for it. This isn't an affiliate program but rather an ad hoc approach that incentivizes people's networking skills. It is important to note you will need a well-structured and streamlined workflow to filter out leads that don't match up. Training in advance, with back-up filters to ensure you get what you want, will yield great returns as you scale.

390. Random massive payout for a referral as a PR hook

Come up with an unbelievable payout, make it easy for people to get involved, and have the rules and structured systems working well. Once you go, use strong public relations to get the word out. Find the top growth hacker and ***get paid $100,000 for doing so***. Have smaller payouts against a scaling system that get others paying money along the way, of course, more than the usual amounts. This incentivizes people to get involved, but for those who do well,

Let's hire the best talent

This exercise helps identify the best hacks to hire talent. This enables you to track performance, re-use top performers, discard poor performers, and create new hacks that might outperform existing ones. Choose hacks you want to use. Write down the number and name of the hack. Once a hack is applied, capture top-level learning points and the result.

Hack | # | Name of hacked
Learning | | What did you learn?
Result | | What are the results?

Hack | # | Name of hacked
Learning | | What did you learn?
Result | | What are the results?

Hack | # | Name of hacked
Learning | | What did you learn?
Result | | What are the results?

Hack | # | Name of hacked
Learning | | What did you learn?
Result | | What are the results?

Hack | # | Name of hacked
Learning | | What did you learn?
Result | | What are the results?

Performance of hacks

Capture, top, and poor performance hiring hacks here. At the same time, generate new hacks by combing existing hiring hacks or using existing hacks to inspire a new hiring hack. Use this performance page to develop your next action plan with your team to outperform your competition in finding, attracting, and retaining top growth talent.

Top performing Hacks

Hack   [#]   Name of hacked _____

Hack   [#]   Name of hacked _____

Hack   [#]   Name of hacked _____

Poor performing Hacks

Hack   [#]   Name of hacked _____

Hack   [#]   Name of hacked _____

Hack   [#]   Name of hacked _____

New Combo Hacks

Hack   [#]   Name of hacked _____   [#]   Name of hacked _____

Hack   [#]   Name of hacked _____   [#]   Name of hacked _____

Hack   [#]   Name of hacked _____   [#]   Name of hacked _____

New generated hacks

Hack   [#]   Name of hacked _____

Hack   [#]   Name of hacked _____

Hack   [#]   Name of hacked _____

get them to share, and those in the network who share it get other incentives so that you have a layer of sharing to make this go viral.

391. Side hustle the open referral program

Want a side hustle? Find those in related industries to recruitment, marketing or other business-related areas that growth hacking can be associated with. Get them onboard to make this low friction and high impact, with great one-time or ongoing income-building oppor-tunities. Get them networking and give them the tools and generous payouts.

392. Free classified ads for open referral program

Find and place ads for free or at low cost on classified ads web-sites, where you can present the opportunity for open recruitment.

393. Multi-level marketing networks hacked

Tap into MLM networks for other products and present this opportu-nity. They are interested in quick money-making opportunities and they network. Although this might be a bit removed from finding growth hackers, you would be tapping into their second and third-degree networks.

394. Franchise business shows to recruit for open referral programs

Find business franchise shows or other related events and recruit from there. Make sure this is known as a business opportunity which anyone can instantly tap into.

395. YouTube video for open referral program

Optimize as a side hustle for those looking to make ad hoc or ongo-ing income. This opens the doors to different lifestyles and people who can open new contacts for your networking. Optimize for side hustle and other related business opportunities.

396. Freelancer website recruitment

Tap into Fiverr.com, UpWork and the likes to find and recruit those who might align or put a post for such an opportunity. The secret is to find those with a business interest, who want to make money, and have an understanding of talent. They don't have to be experts; they simply have to be able to network and work hard. This is an open referral program. However, it's important to have filters and guidelines and keep things simple.

397. Use transactional emails to recruit open referrals

Use your frequent transactional emails to recruit people who would be interested in your open referral program. Remember, open means that any one can get involved, and it can be just on referral or on an ad hoc basis. This low-friction and high-impact approach widens the network of possible recruiters, or people who are not re-cruiters but who can open your funnel to find growth hackers.

398. Hiring affiliate program

Now you can set up an affiliate program for non-recruiters to create ongoing income for themselves. They will network for you and pre-qualify talent. They get paid for doing this for you. Very simple.

399. Join other affiliate networks

Join other affiliate programs and recruit affiliates internally. This is simple. Just tap in, get networking and informally present this alternative opportunity to top-performing affiliates. At the same time, there are affiliate programs that are open to other opportunities and those you can work with explicitly.

400. Recruit from other affiliate networks

Work within the community support networks in affiliate programs and recruit outright. Now, this is sensitive as it can be seen as spam and against community guidelines. Hence, you need to work very quietly and in such a way that you cannot be detected.

401. Position your program as a business opportunity

Show the income earning power and how that can change the lives of those who join. People want the result that transforms them, not the efforts they need to make. Use those opportunities to showcase your affiliate program as a business opportunity. The secret to this is using business opportunity or franchise-style shows to get your opportunity inside there.

402. Feature your top performers in other networks

Use your top performers as a means to attract others. Showcase them to other affiliate networks to get their attention and get them into your affiliate program.

403. YouTube affiliate videos

Build a series of videos to attract affiliate members. This can cover who has made significant income and at what levels. Explain what is involved and address the basics that anyone might like to know.

This way, your recruitment process for your affiliate program is on autopilot. Be sure to use a direct call to action in the description and video content to register interested parties into your program.

404. Email newsletter recruitment

Use your email newsletter to recruit affiliates. Have ongoing, passive and lead-prominent content positioned for the program in the newsletter. At the same time, have some dedicated content that is more prominent at times that make sense and don't interrupt your other content flows.

405. Landing page for affiliate program

Include a dedicated section within the hiring landing page for affiliates. This will need to have more information to address the program and operate it. Use the landing page as a gateway and eventually have your own dedicated sub-landing page for the affiliate program itself.

406. Pay other recruiters

Find other recruiters, and create both ad hoc payments, and affiliate payment programs for them. This is where they network but spend more time on the pre-qualification part, saving you more time and effort. It's worth the investment, as they take on the risk of time and effort investment, but it also incentivizes their networking.

407. Go to recruitment events and conferences

Recruitment events may not be a direct interest, but those in the recruiting business will be there and this is a great opportunity to recruit the recruiters themselves into your recruitment programs.

408. Ask other growth hackers who recruited them

Tap into growth hackers in other organizations and ask which recruiter was the one who recruited them. They may introduce you to other recruiters who they have met but not had success with. Take on all those referrals and recruit the recruiters themselves.

409. Outreach to the big guys

Find the top recruiters, even if they are in another field, and design a proposition for them. Hiring an external recruiter isn't easy if they have a strong success record. You need to attract them with little risk, easy pay and a big opportunity. Think this through and outreach. Although this might feel farfetched, you might be surprised how many may sign up and who may refer you to other recruiters you can recruit into your referral program.

410. Outreach to former recruiters

Find recruiters who used to work for the big guys. They might be in a very potent position to accept an invitation to join your referral program. They may see this as a bridging opportunity or a whole new channel for them in the next steps of their career. Position for both possibilities and get them onboard.

411. Recruit recruiters on social media

Put out a post that you're hiring, or have an event for recruiters. Use your social media reach to attract recruiters who can recruit and get them into your referral program.

412. Place a job post for recruiters

A job post can also help. Be sure to state it's a commission- or affili-ate-related income. The difference is the type of recruiters who will take on such opportunities.

413. Student side hustle

Get students to earn a side income as they go through school. You will need to train them in how to recruit and give them the tools and guidelines, but they will be motivated to get out there and find your next best growth hacker and get paid.

414. Events and conferences

Event planners go a long way to recruit the top minds for their events. Although you might be tempted to go for people they di-rectly promote, and you should, it's those who accompany them who might be of greater interest to you.

415. Speakers for hire

Speakers come with ideas, credentials and new perspectives. They can be potential new hires. They might be more senior hires, or even on an advisory level, but their work and exposure can be very valuable to your growth.

416. Ask placement questions live

At their talk, if they offer a question-and-answer session, ask them hypothetical questions. Ask, for example, if you were the head of growth for our company or a specific situation, what would you do…? This helps to pick their brain, of course, but it also places in their mind the idea of working with you.

417. Outreach in advance to speakers

Reach out to the speaker in advance and request a one-to-one meeting at the event. If that doesn't work, you will be there and would like a 3-minute handshake introduction. Want to go further? You can state your interest in hiring them and that you would like to meet them at the event on an informal basis, to get to know them.

418. Auto-like and comment on speakers' platforms

Want to create an impression? Start by creating value with passive support on their own social content. The secret to this is that it shows your interest with little effort. This paves the way to future discussions with the speaker, and even introductions.

419. Invite them to speak after the event

Engage the speaker for another speaking event. Hire them from that event to speak, either at a smaller event related to that event, or a completely different event. The point is that you hire them for something else, unrelated, but use that event to meet them. The secret to this is getting them engaged and tapping into their expertise and network. And, of course, eventually, if they are of interest and fit, hiring them onto your team.

420. Invite them to an after-party

Throw an after-party, or, if you're joining another one, invite the speaker. This is a great way to get an informal rapport in place. This gives you the ability to tap into them directly and to tap indirectly into their audience and network.

421. Invite them for a one-to-one coffee

Since they will be at the event, carve out 15 minutes to have a coffee at the event itself. This way, you have a dedicated one-to-one time, without wasting their time or yours. This gives you an informal path to recruiting them or tapping into their network.

422. Panelists as experts

If they are not speaking, they might be on a panel. Go to the panel, hear their ideas and recruit. Like the speakers, this can be more senior people and their network, and resources might be more variable than the direct skills you're seeking. Tap into them wisely.

423. Tell your audience in advance

Let your audience know in advance. Very simply, announce the panel to your email list, social media and other channels. Use this as an opportunity to recruit participants. The secret behind this is to show the value you bring to the event and conference, but also to be able to tap into your audience's network.

424. Have a pre-promoted surprise or giveaway

Want to get the attention of those who matter? Announce a surprise or, even better, a giveaway. You don't have to do this in a cheesy way, but in keeping with the topic, the agenda and the event. Give it a high value that shows you bring value to the event. The secret to this is to give away something that would attract growth hackers.

425. Showcase your cases

Be armed with your top case studies. Use your top growth hacking case studies to drive value to the audience and event organizers but, more importantly, to attract growth hackers. Draw on cases that would get growth hackers interested in wanting to know more, and in becoming a part of the teams that develop such amazing growth hacks.

426. Talk about how great your team and workplace is

Plug your team, your work culture and workplace dynamics. Use this as a way to draw on attractive attributes that would naturally appeal to growth hackers. For example, advertise the fact that we give your growth hackers *25% of their time off to be creative* and come up with some of the most mind-blowing growth hacking ideas. Give those examples and their impact. The secret to this is injecting into the minds of potential growth hackers on your team that they would want to be part of such a team.

427. Become the moderator, not the expert

Don't want to be the one answering the questions? Become the one who drives the questions. Use this plug-in opportunity via your introduction to talk about growth hacking and your team. At the same time, inject questions about growth hacking, and the working environment for growth hackers. When they all answer, you can inject into the conversation to explain what you do at your firm, then ask whether they do something similar. If not, ask how they would go about this.

428. Announce panel session on chatbot

Use your chatbot wisely, both on your main website, and on your growth hacking hiring page. This way, you can get a mailing list of interested parties and get them to follow your content. The secret to this is reaching out to audiences and their networks, beyond those who would directly attend the event or conference.

429. Record the session and promote it afterwards

Use this opportunity to tap into people afterwards. Highlight key messages into short content to place on YouTube Shorts and Tik-Tok etc. This way, smaller, bite-size clips with key messages can get people more interested. Use a call to action in the description to get direct hires.

430. Go live on social media

With the permission of your event and conference organizer, of course, go live on social. Stream the session and have your own producer at your end to highlight key messages and clip short form content live. The secret is to show your existing audience you're active, motivate your affiliate networks and attract future hires. Use a direct call to action for direct hires, whether it be an open live position or just open application format.

431. Walk around

Yes, it's time to take a walk. It's random and not so well-structured, but there is a chance of this working. Get targeted by hanging around those sessions and talks that attract the talent you want to hire. Ask questions in panel sessions and it might be a good idea to ask growth hacker hiring questions. This might flag you up as a recruiter but, as you move around, this helps you to filter your discussions.

432. Meeting spot for pre-set quick meetings

Set a spot at a certain time at an event to meet everyone and ensure it's visible. Want to take this one step further? Take a sign to hold up, a bit like a tourist guide, to keep the crowd together. It feels cheesy but it gets everyone organized and asking what this is. Get potential future recruits to meet you at the event or conference at that point with others as well.

433. Coffee shop on the outside

Find a coffee shop or meeting place outside the venue and own it. Sit down and use this spot as your outside meeting spot to gather those you want to have pre-arranged meetings with in advance. Be the one who introduces and use this as an informal method to get to know future recruits.

434. Social media posting to call your spot

Use a social media post and campaign to drive those whom you have not reached out to, who will be attending the event or conference, to meet you and the team at a certain point at a specific time. Be sure to use mentions and hashtags for the event itself, to trend on their traffic.

435. Go live while taking the walk

Take that walk around live. Get others on your social network to virtually meet with you but, more importantly, get those whom you meet to introduce themselves and get excited about being featured on your social platforms. This way, you can mention them and grab them into your lists. You can also reach out later and recruit or get referrals.

436. Walk around with someone famous

This idea is very simple: find a well-known growth hacker or business personality and pay them to walk around with you. The secret behind this is to get the pulling power of someone famous – and you don't need someone very famous, either; someone with enough pulling power. Then agree with this person to ensure introductions so that as they get people coming to them, they will introduce you and your team.

437. Virtual networking

There are many ways to find people at a virtual event. Their names are exposed and in some cases even their social handles. Use this to get into theory networks. There are two opportunities: one is directly with them; and the other is indirectly, by tapping into their network.

438. Find virtual events on event and community sites

Create alerts and frequently scan event and community platforms. The good news is there are many of them and you can tap into even smaller events you might never have considered or even known that they exist.

439. Tap into growth hacking community calls

Growth hacking communities organize their own internal calls. Whether they are training, or just discussions, get on alert and get into those calls. The secret behind this is to be an active member and show interest.

440. Create a Google alert to find and tap into virtual events

Google alerts can do all the work for you. Be sure to use the right keywords and create a few alerts, not just one. Focus on keywords such as "virtual event", "online virtual event", "online event" and then add in the topic to the keywords. Obviously, you will use "growth hack", "growth hacking" and "growth hackers" but you will need some broader terms as well, such as "growth marketing" and "digital marketing", anywhere others may be roaming around. Also, create keywords around key personalities and known events to be alerted and ahead of the curve.

441. Tap into your interns to find virtual events

Get your interns to find you those events. They can do the research but, more importantly, you can tap into their networks and think broader and out of the box to find potential virtual events to tap into. The secret here is that they will have access to ideas and networks you did not know about, which helps you tap into the younger, more dynamic talent you need.

442. Tap into your recruitment affiliate network for virtual events

Use your affiliate recruitment network if you have one, or are building one. Let them create a list in which everyone participates, so they can all help each other out. This is a simple Google sheet to post the event on there with a few details; this way, everyone can keep ahead of the curve.

443. Tap into growth hacking course instructors

Find top growth hacking courses online and track down the instructors. See if they are creating virtual events or attending or even mentioning other virtual events. The secret behind this is, they will be in the know, so tap into their know-how.

444. Job boards and their events

Follow the main job boards out there, and simply participate in their broader events. Use this as a platform to network a bit deeper and find talent in nearby areas. The secret behind this is to open new possible channels you did not know about to find growth hackers.

445. Educational institute virtual events

This is a bit old-school , but educational institutes are also trying to tap into virtual events. They are most likely creating their own or participating in one. The secret behind this is to tap into them and their networks.

446. After-parties

Every event has some kind of an after-party. Find it, as this is where real networking happens. Usually, these are less formal and invite-only, but they are not impossible to penetrate. Get in, and network.

447. Brand your own after-party and push it

Make your own 'hire a growth hacker' party. This will attract growth hackers, but also those involved in the ecosystem, which can also be very helpful. The secret behind this is being explicit and refining your audience to those you want and explaining your reasons.

448. Invite the media from the media center

Tap into the media center set up by the conference and event organization. Get the full list of media members, and give them a unique, limited-time invite to the after-party. Be sure to tell them it's for growth hackers and it's a unique opportunity to tap into this community. A ton of stories can come out of this. The secret behind this is to tap into the media, and get them to tell your story; this enables you to get more growth hackers into your ecosystem for hiring purposes.

449. Invite the speakers and panelists get it rolling

Reach out and go beyond. Get the speakers and panelists to show up. Here is the secret: once they commit, they use their presence as a hook to get others to come. After all, they will be at the event, so why not come on over to the after-party, right?

450. Get event sponsors involved in your party

Want to get your party paid for? Pitch the existing sponsors who are already invested in the event. Let them be part of the party and the benefits of an after-party. The secret behind this is that after-parties don't have to be as expensive as their full-on sponsorship in the event. This also helps them to realize that their initial investment in the event allows them to also create meaningful connections, in a better setting.

451. Get a mentor to host the party

Get a well-known growth hacker, mentor or coach to host the party. Let them be the magnet to bring in the interest of the audience. The secret is tapping into other audiences and their networks within the space itself.

452. Give an award at the party

Use the party to give awards. This is a great way to get your top players in the growth hacking space into one place at one time, and those who want to be part of this will want to meet them. The secret is to get those winners out and to get to know them to see if you can recruit them; at the same time, they will attract growth hackers from their network that you can tap into to hire.

453. Get the party on to LinkedIn Live

Go live on LinkedIn. Most Lives on LinkedIn are dry and boring. Get your LinkedIn page sparkling with new forms of energy. Get the party going live; this way, you can tap into people who mention the party or who are attending, so you can directly tap into their network. The secret is to get someone on your team to reach out and connect with those who attend or mention or comment as you broadcast.

454. Invite your top performers

Get your top performers out; they will socially bring other top performers you have not yet met. Get to know them and see if you can recruit them. The secret behind this is in tapping your own top performers' networks to get new recruits. Do not forget to tap into your own industry contacts.

455. Invite your affiliate network of recruiters

Get your affiliate network of recruiters to the party to create a better rapport with them but let them tap into the audience and recruit on the spot for you. The secret behind this is tapping into connectors to uncover deeper networks of hidden talent.

456. Invite your interns to party

Give your interns the benefit of having a party. They will like it, and allow them to invite others who are also in the growth hacking space. The secret behind this is to tap into their networks on the spot.

457. Throw a party

Can't get invited? Throw your own party connected to the event. The organizer may not like this, but they can't stop you. This happens all the time, especially where events have mega procurement opportunities. Use their drive to bring the right talent to your party. In fact, it can be a growth hacker party for this specific industry and the topic being highlighted at that event.

458. Set an Eventbrite pre-event to get participants

Use Eventbrite search engine to tap into their audience. But here's the secret: name your part of the big event or conference to get people who are going to that event into your after-party. Make it exclusive and limited, and yes, state that it's for growth hackers. You will get others who want to join; get them into the party too. The secret behind this is that it's an informal mechanism to network and building relationships.

459. Use Meetup to get your side-party going

Like Eventbrite, Meetup and the likes are powerful, but they have the added benefit of community and SEO power. Using their community power, you can tap into other communities and get them to share your after-party at a big event, like you're going to TechCrunch Disrupt, and you're having an exclusive growth hackers' after-party. That gets attention and you should use it wisely. The secret behind this is tapping into other audiences to unlock hidden networks of talent.

460. Broadcast that party, man!

Get your party on social media and live. You don't have to show all, but enough to get those who did not make it interested enough to get on a mailing list for future networking opportunities. This way, you can tap into your audience and those generated from the event. The secret here is FOMO (fear of missing out) and using that to build a mailing list to be used for direct and indirect recruitment purposes.

461. Host it at your hacker house

Got your hacker house set up? There's no better place to host a party than there. In fact, this will get the attention of those who you united. Logistically, this might be a bit challenging, but if you can pull this off, do it. The secret behind this is rapport building, to softly identify top talent.

462. Get a celeb to host your party

Get someone famous to show up. A famous growth hacker would be a good idea, or if you can't get one, find a famous business per-sonality. Sometimes, social media influencers can be of interest, too. The secret here is you need a hook, and there's no better way than people wanting to meet someone famous.

463. Get that party into your email signature

Want more interest? Use your email signatures across the organi-zation to announce your party. This is for a short period only but it gets people excited. The secret here is to use this underutilized piece of real estate to get traffic.

464. Get those videos about the party on your YouTube channel

Get the video out there. The secret here is FOMO (fear of missing out), and making those who did not attend want to be part of the next one. And yes, you should have a call to action to join a mailing list to be invited to the next one. Use that list wisely.

465. Use your chatbots to announce the party

Use a chatbot, both on your main website and on your dedicated growth hacking hiring landing page, to announce the party and to get people to come to the event. The secret behind this is that if they don't make it, allow them to get highlighted afterwards so you don't lose that opportunity to connect with them.

466. Sponsor a fringe activity

Partner up with the event organizer and make a mini-event within theirs. Think of it like a growth hacking activity based on the topic and agenda of that event. It's a nice spotlight for the event orga-nizer, and you can create a sponsorship top-up opportunity. You can take a social responsibility angle as well; this can tap into softer and more meaningful reasons for the fringe activity.

467. Gamify a unique fringe activity

A fringe activity by nature will attract attention if it's well designed. Gamify the hell out of it and get others within the event who are not directly related to get involved. This is about getting the attention of existing participants into your fringe activity. The secret is to lever-age the power of reach and bring them into your mindset, and at-tract growth hackers. Make the fringe activity growth-related.

468. Make the fringe activity a contest

Give away a big prize with pre-qqualifications. There's no better way than giving away something amazing, like a car or a lot of cash. You will have attention and interest. Remember, your leads may not be growth hackers, but capture them anyway. The secret behind this is to reach out to them later for tapping into. Making the fringe activity growth hacking-related helps filter and get the right audience in place.

469. Leverage media center for fringe activity

Really well-organized conferences and events will have a media center. This is where members of the media get together for convergence purposes with some cool perks. Get into this media center, even if you register as a member of the media. If you cannot get it, don't worry; you can still access them. The secret is to pitch them the fringe activity and get them involved as well.

470. Put secret envelopes under chairs as part of a fringe activity

Get your unique fringe activity under everyone. Put secret envelopes under their seats as part of gamifying participation. This way, you get the attention of every attendee. The secret here as well is to capture leads via interest and filter later.

471. Spin that wheel to boost fringe activity

Build a physical or virtual wheel spinner. Make the winnings related to your product offering. Use this to collect leads as well and filter later. The secret behind this is engagement and generating new leads. This is a form of gamifying the experience in a fun way.

472. Get a really weird celebrity for your fringe activity

Hire a very outspoken celebrity as part of your fringe activity to get attention and leads. Capture those leads and filter later. This can be for both direct and indirect hiring purposes. The secret behind this is getting attention and tapping into hidden networks within your audience.

473. Participate as a speaker

Send your head of growth as a speaker. Growth hackers want to network with other growth hackers and this is a great way of getting them out of their dark corners. What is interesting is being industry- and topic-specific, using the events agenda. This helps refine and define some of the talent you might be looking for right in front of you.

474. Bring on that reality show

Get your speaker and speaking session as part of your reality show. A reality show can go a long way, as can using your expertise power. The secret here is leveraging the event and conference audience.

475. Bring on those amazing facts and figures

Use live, juicy and native growth cases. Let others know what you're up to. You don't have to tell all, but enough to gain interest. The secret to this is, it's not just amazing content and something for speakers to leverage but to attract talent. Attracting talent is about showing you're ahead of the curve and this is what top growth hackers want.

476. Bring on the big party

Throw a party after the event or conference and mention this as part of the speaker's content. This points to a call to action that attracts growth hackers from the get-go. The secret is to use the event and conferences platform to hijack traffic towards your party, where growth hackers can network.

477. Tap into participants and leverage their network

Find out who is attending. This includes all those participating, sponsors and even exhibitors, if any. Leverage them in advance. Announce your speaking session by reaching out in advance. Use this opportunity to leverage them and their network to a source. You will need a call to action as a source, like a party, a report, another event or something of value to get them interested. The secret behind this is to leverage their audience when they talk about it. It's a lighter, softer approach, but it's about tapping into other networks.

478. Announce a speaker session via the growth hacking community

Tap into existing growth hacking communities and announce the speaking opportunity. Although many of them may not join or take part, get them to sign up on an email list to send them the talk afterwards. The secret behind this is to generate a list of potential leads. Do this in conjunction with community leaders so it's not seen as spam.

479. Get affiliate networks of recruiters to promote speaking session

Leverage your affiliate network to push content. This helps them attract people within their network for recruitment purposes. The secret behind this is to support your affiliate program members who are out recruiting for you.

480. Get speaker videos on hiring dedicated landing page

Use that dedicated landing page for hiring growth hackers. Get speaker videos and other content up there to show an active push toward attracting talent. The secret behind this is, engage your audience with quality content and draw them into your hiring funnel.

481. Get the speaker session into your email signature and newsletter

Use your email signature and newsletters to announce speaker sessions. At the same time, once you have the video ready, provide access so those who did not attend can watch it later on. The secret behind this is keeping top-of-mind.

482. Post speaking session via YouTube

Simply use the speaker session as content to be posted on YouTube and use this as a direct call to action to work for the growth team. The secret behind this is awareness and lead generation.

483. Message on chatbot to see speaking session

Get your chatbots, both on your dedicated hiring page and general website, to announce the speaking session and finally the video of the session itself. The secret behind this is to get interested talent to see your speaking engagement and approach.

484. Clone your growth hackers

If it works, repeat it. Easier said than done, but having a formal cloning program might be the right approach. A cloning program induces growth hackers into your growth culture and ensures the skill sets needed are fine-tuned.

485. Internship program

A classic internship program can work. The difference is being focused on growth exclusively. This enables you to attract and retain the exact skill sets you want. Growth hackers are not accustomed to such programs, although they may be a classic approach. Sometimes old tricks with new applications can be very effective.

486. Get your internship program sponsored by someone famous

Get someone famous onboard. But do not use someone within the growth hacking space. The secret to this is using wider appeal to narrow your interest. For example, have a significant business influencer who can comment on results from a practical perspective. The secret to this is tapping into a social responsibility and social impact strategy to get business community leaders involved in your internship program.

487. Gamify your internship program

Gamify the internship experience. Create levels over time, and badges with points, and announce them as they move through your program. Use this to get them social and push virtuality by sharing this in their own networks. The secret behind this is getting your interest excited and engaged, especially younger dynamic talent, and getting them to tap into their network to help you get more interns.

Let's hire the best talent

This exercise helps identify the best hacks to hire talent. This enables you to track performance, re-use top performers, discard poor performers, and create new hacks that might outperform existing ones. Choose hacks you want to use. Write down the number and name of the hack. Once a hack is applied, capture top-level learning points and the result.

Hack [#] Name of hacked

Learning [ ] What did you learn?

Result [ ] What are the results?

Hack [#] Name of hacked

Learning [ ] What did you learn?

Result [ ] What are the results?

Hack [#] Name of hacked

Learning [ ] What did you learn?

Result [ ] What are the results?

Hack [#] Name of hacked

Learning [ ] What did you learn?

Result [ ] What are the results?

Hack [#] Name of hacked

Learning [ ] What did you learn?

Result [ ] What are the results?

Performance of hacks

Capture, top, and poor performance hiring hacks here. At the same time, generate new hacks by combing existing hiring hacks or using existing hacks to inspire a new hiring hack. Use this performance page to develop your next action plan with your team to outperform your competition in finding, attracting, and retaining top growth talent.

Top performing Hacks

Hack   [#]   Name of hacked _____

Hack   [#]   Name of hacked _____

Hack   [#]   Name of hacked _____

Poor performing Hacks

Hack   [#]   Name of hacked _____

Hack   [#]   Name of hacked _____

Hack   [#]   Name of hacked _____

New Combo Hacks

Hack   [#]   Name of hacked _____   [#]   Name of hacked _____

Hack   [#]   Name of hacked _____   [#]   Name of hacked _____

Hack   [#]   Name of hacked _____   [#]   Name of hacked _____

New generated hacks

Hack   [#]   Name of hacked _____

Hack   [#]   Name of hacked _____

Hack   [#]   Name of hacked _____

488. Get interns to story tell

Story-tell the hell out of their experience with your organization. Get interns to use the power of social media to tell the story of their experience, especially learnings, inspirations etc. The secret is using social media to get attention, and eventually become viral among potential young growth hackers. This is especially appealing to those considering the field and wanting to enter into the growth hacking space.

489. Give interns awards

Massage the egos of your interns. Give them awards and let them broadcast it. The secret is to create many categories to have several winners. This gives them a boost, as well as showing to external and future growth hackers the importance of recognizing talent.

490. Get interns making paid referrals

Pay interns to get your more interns. Of course, you need to be very succinct and clear on qualifications. The secret to this is doing it closer to the middle of your program. This means they have got a taste of what is required and that way they are more likely to get you better potential growth hacker recruits.

491. Get interns on your reality show

Combine your internship program and a reality show. It is not about having a dedicated show but rather an episode or segment for interns only. This helps combine your efforts; a reality show can reveal other parts of your talent acquisition strategy for growth hackers. The secret behind this is generating new hiring leads into your funnel.

492. Recruit interns via email signature

This is simple, but we need to cover the simple stuff. Use your email signatures across the whole entity to drive traffic to recruiting interns. The secret behind this is to tap into your existing network for recruitment leads.

493. Recruit interns via chatbots

Another simple one is to use chatbots to recruit interns. This can be on your dedicated landing pages for hiring growth hackers as well but also on your main website pages. The secret behind this is to tap into web traffic and get them into your hiring funnel.

494. Apprentice program

Sit alongside and copy; a very simple, old-school system and it works. In fact, it's more effective than formal training or recruiting from formally educated sources. Why? Because it enables the real application of skills, the fast development of underperforming skills, and cultivating their international skills into your environment. Set up a formal program, and have a 1:3 or 1:5 ratio program, meaning that one of your employees can have 3 to 5 people working alongside them.

495. Hack of the week

Use your apprentice program to generate ads highlighting hacks used during their program. Get those highlights out there, on YouTube and other social media. Do not give it all away, of course. The secret here is highlighting a desirable apprenticeship program so that other growth hackers want to get into it. Remember, the apprenticeship program is designed to help you test and develop talent into your main growth team.

496. Blog post top hacks

Take those top hacks developed in your apprenticeship program and turn them into blog posts. The secret here is to use their capabilities to explain their hacks to others in a clear and concise way. Using a blog post, you're able to get engagement to test and validate their ideas. More importantly, use it as a recruitment channel into the growth team itself.

497. Apprentice journey from A to Z

Like a reality show, highlight the story of the apprentice. It doesn't have to be a massive production. It can be several simple 60-second videos over a period of time. The secret behind this is direct feedback internally, but it also attracts other growth hackers externally.

498. Get mentors and coaches on to the apprentice program

Get those amazing growth mentors and coaches into your apprentice program. Use their reach and influence to attract attention to your apprentice program and drive traffic towards it. The secret behind this is ego massaging. It simply works.

499. Get celebrities on to your apprentice program

Find business celebrities and influencers to join an episode of your apprentice program or have them as part of a judging panel. Use their audience pulling power to drive more interest toward your apprentice program. The secret behind this is getting a broader influence than someone in the growth hacking space, such as a client who would be the receiver of the growth hacking results.

500. Apprentice growth hacking community

Tap into existing growth hacking communities, and place apprentice program content directly inside. Use this as part of being in that community, not spam. Work with community leaders to drive this content as well. The idea is to position this as a learning opportunity. The secret is that naturally the best talent will rise, from a desire to be part of your apprentice program, or to directly apply to a growth hacking position at your organization.

501. Apprentice awards to others

Use the attention to the apprentice program to drive awards to others. In other words, when you identify growth hackers outside your network and you want to give them an award, make it part of your apprentice program. The secret behind this is to show that their talent is being admired by others growing in the industry, which is true, but a powerful hook.

502. Apprentice hacker house

Create a hacker house and simply run your apprentice program from there. Use the hacker house format as a way to house your apprentice program. This enables you to have long-term programs and a more interesting appeal to your audience. The secret to this is appealing to younger, more dynamic growth hackers who are looking for more than just a job but also want somewhere to belong and be part of something.

503. Apprentice after-parties

Use conferences and events to develop your own after-parties and get your apprentice program into this. In other words, get your apprentices to events and conferences, but into the after-party where the real networking and growth happens. The secret behind this is to attract other growth hackers who want to network.

504. Apprentice program on dedicated landing page

It seems obvious, but it's always important to remember to include your apprentice program and all of its content on your dedicated growth hacking hiring page. The secret behind this is to promote and generate direct leads from your website into your apprentice program.

505. Put the apprentice program on YouTube

Push your apprentice program onto YouTube, both on Live as an event and as recorded videos for others to watch later. The secret behind this is to optimize your apprentice program YouTube videos to continuously attract new traffic and, eventually, qualified leads.

506. Reality show

Want to get more creative? Take your apprentice program and stream it. Attract others from within the audience who show an interest for your apprentice program and recruit. The secret behind this is to stretch way beyond your four walls and tap into dark corners where you would not normally find talent.

507. Use the reality show to showcase mentors to attract talent

Get those growth mentors you hire or bring on, onto your show. It's a great exposure point for mentors and coaches and a way to create more content. However, the big secret here is to show credibility and drive interest from future growth hackers on your team. This is a BIG FOMO (fear of missing out) approach and it works.

508. Social media the hell out of your reality show

Get the reality show all over social media. Use viral loops to get people on your team, in your audience and even customers who support your brand sharing. The secret to this is getting within the layer of networks you have touched. By doing this, you drive interest but also accumulate a wide range of access to potential talent. This may distract from the show so ensure you have a reality show pipeline separate to this.

509. Reality show awards - massage their egos

Let's get massaging egos. Use your network to award growth hackers who are not on your team as a way to attract them. Giving them amazing exposure is the big secret here. This exposure makes them more loyal to your brand and gives them the feeling that they owe you something. This can be used wisely, not just to hire them directly, but to get them to open their networks to getting the best growth hackers.

510. Reality show virtual coffee day

Use an episode to combine a virtual coffee day with your top decision-makers. Why? The big secret here is showing your leadership is genuinely interested in the growth of their organization and appreciate growth hacking. This gives future growth hackers a sense of wanting to belong and that is the secret behind this.

511. Hacker house reality show party

Get that hacker house moving. Integrate your own, a sponsored or another hacker house party into your reality show. The secret here is that they want to party with the top growth hackers too. Remember, since many growth hackers have been dislodged from each other thanks to fragmentation, they naturally want to get with the best in the field. There's no better way to show it and use it as a recruitment tool.

512. Get your interns on the reality show

Get your interns working harder but having fun. Give them some exposure and a chance to give a testimonial in the form of storytelling. The secret behind this is it shows new, younger growth hackers they can belong and be part of such a team. Get them to emphasize their desires to be part of the growth team and why, and then to explain how they have been nurtured and supported.

513. Give 25% time off and get that on the reality show

Give your existing growth hackers 25% time off for thinking and developing new ideas and make it part of the reality show. It can be a segment, or a sub-segment, to show the culture of growth development. Why? The secret behind is helping your audience to understand the importance of self-development and how you support this as an organization.

514. Headlines and hooks into your signature for your reality show

Use those email signatures wisely. Use your top hooks, catch-phrases, results or something of massive interest in your signature. Consider something like this: "Did you see last night's 25x hack?" Put this with a call to action, watch and learn. The secret behind this is to get the interest of your direct contacts and then tap into their networks.

515. Use your chatbot to make your reality show popular

Drop messages in those chatbots that get those who want to join your team watching the reality show. The secret here is twofold; it gets them more interested, but also it enables them to tell their networks and get more growth hackers into your ecosystem.

516. F%$# growth hacks

Just as success is popular, so are massive mistakes. Either create a whole episode or just a segment within your reality show and focus on massive mistakes. The secret behind this is learning. Great talent learn as much from mistakes as they do from successes but highlighting this in a unique and fun way can be very attractive to future recruits.

517. Bridging training and job placement

If you're curating formal training programs, build a bridging program. The apprentice approach is great and combining it with a reality show can be even more powerful; it needs to be very creative as this can be an ongoing program that will yield high returns on investment in terms of talent and talent attraction.

518. Go to other training courses and recruit

Simply go into other training courses, and other training-style programs. Be a student, but be there to network and find talent and recruit. The secret behind this is to go covert, and recruit from within.

519. Sign up via online events to get access to participants

Many online events and training programs have an online element and in many cases you may be able to see everyone who is signed up. It may not be right away; you might have to join and then tap into them. However, some tools show who is coming, to get you motivated and to share. The secret behind this is that their participants are exposed. Track them down, research them and recruit.

520. Track testimonials from trainings and recruit

Trainees sharing reviews and comments openly is a great breeding ground. Research them, find them and see if they are a fit. If they are not a fit, simply ask for a referral and use their network to find new growth hackers. The secret behind this is creating referrals into the hiring funnel.

521. Get your bridging strategy on your dedicated landing page

Do not forget to use your dedicated landing page wisely. Put any bridging programs or strategies you will be running on the dedicated landing page. Bridging programs include your intern, or apprentice programs and so on. The secret behind this is to create more than one entry point for new talent.

522. Highlight compensation for highly successful growth hacks

Want those you're bridging to be motivated? There's no better way than to show them a carrot at the end of the stick. This is a way of motivating future growth hackers on how top performers get compensated. The secret behind this is to give them motivation but also a desire to be part of your growth hacking team.

523. Create a new revenue stream for course content creators

Aside from their challenges of creating income on their courses, create an affiliate program to help compensate them for recruiters as referrals. The secret behind this is to introduce a new, lucrative income stream for course creators to attract and place new recruits.

524. Pull out the golden cuffs

Letting future recruits know about perks and benefits upfront naturally gravitates them towards you. Everyone wants to work for an awesome company. However, that has changed a lot, especially after the COVID-19 pandemic and thanks to the great resignation.

525. Training and development included

Pay for all top-up training once on-boarded. Do not stop training; allow growth hackers to expand their multi-skills so they become more crossfunctional-oriented.

526. Use training and development to generate articles

Got your team on an amazing training and development program? Get them to write blog articles to attract others by putting reviews and observations on the training. The secret here is to capture outcomes and learnings and turn them into content. Using this content, you can attract growth hackers who are always seeking the latest and greatest in the growth hacking field.

527. Use outcomes from training for speaking opportunities

Got some amazing learning outcomes from training? Convert these to speaking opportunities. Take those learning outcomes and turn them into speaking content to be placed at events and conferences. By doing this, you are creating new, cutting-edge content by driving it through a speech. The secret behind this is enabling your internal team to get motivated and recognized, but more importantly, you're attracting the top minds using the latest and greatest developments.

528. Develop a train the trainer program

Get your team to take training, then deploy it internally. This helps the development of the overall team but also shows future growth hacker hires that you have a development program to take them to the next level. The secret behind this is to get traction with your content, both on your dedicated landing page and also social media content.

529. Create a course development program

Take all those learning outcomes, and put together a program for your team to develop their own courses internally. The secret is to ensure they are unique, not a copy of what is already out there. This way, you have a unique category course content. This can be used in many ways; the best way is to get it out in public to attract growth hackers. This can be as simple as putting them up for free on YouTube and having a call to action to get hired.

530. Micro-courses in short-form format

Harness the power of Tiktok, YouTube Shorts, Instagram and other channels to create micro-courses. These micro-courses should be geared towards teaching small, quick skills, to give some challenges, tips and access to resources. The secret behind this is to brand the micro-courses, and have a call to action towards recruitment.

531. Remote and co-working options

They want to work on the beach or from home. Who cares? As long as they get the results and are able to work with the team, let it happen. In fact, it would be wise to encourage it so they can find work/life balance while doing their magic.

532. Go live while co-working or remote

Use social media to promote co-working and remote locations and work styles. Run campaigns on a periodic basis, featuring your growth hackers but also showing their remote work or co-working space. This allows them to highlight the benefits for them and specifically as a growth hacker. The secret behind this is twofold; the first is to get your audience interested in general about your organization. The second is to attract growth hackers who want to be part of this work format.

533. Push your remote and co-working program on the landing page

Show your remote and co-working programs as a benefit to attract new growth hackers. Use your landing page to show this, as well as your translational emails. The secret behind this is that this benefit appeals to younger, more dynamic talent.

534. Tap into local communities while working remotely and co-working

While going to new locations, get tapped into those communities. If your growth hackers are traveling to a new area or city, pre-tap into those communities. Let growth hackers in those localities know someone is coming out and there can be some coffee time scheduled or another way to connect. The secret behind this is to identify new forms of talent in other areas while remote and co-working.

535. Get interns remote and co-working from day one

Don't keep this for just your best growth hackers. Get your intern on the program right away. This will present some management challenges initially. However, if they can perform within such a format, this shows another side to their dynamic capabilities. This is also very appealing to younger, more dynamic talent. The secret behind this is to leverage attention from other growth hackers who would like this type of working format.

536. Use hacker houses as a remote and co-working space

Whether you create, join or sponsor a hacker house, it's a great place to put your talent. This is a place where they can work remotely, and co-work with others. However, the secret here is to network, find new growth hackers and bring them into the fold. This allows you to see them in action before taking them on and test their interest levels.

537. Sponsor the set-up of a home studio

Get your team who are responsible for content creation to set up their own home-made professionals studio. A good set-up doesn't cost much nowadays, and you can produce very good quality content with a home studio. The secret behind this is to inspire and source your team in a structured way to create content and have all the fun tools at their disposal. By doing this, it gives you a lot of content to promote your brand and this can be used to help recruit future candidates.

538. 25% thinking time off

Give compensated time off as part of the job role to be creative and invent. Let them explore other things. This allows them to do their job better. A format of thinking and talent development sounds wise but lacks creativity. If you want to solve big growth problems, get them thinking outside of the box. The secret behind this is that there is no better way than it being part of the job itself rather than additional efforts.

539. Dedicated landing page to feature growth hacks

Highlight the successful and interesting growth hacks generated and feature them on the dedicated landing page. The secret behind this is to show future growth hackers who may join or want to see some of the very cool things happening to attract them.

540. Using the 25% time off while working remotely

Combine your remote working methods to allow the 25% time off as a way to generate new ideas. Remember, there are two goals here. The first is to get your existing growth hackers to develop next-level stuff. The second is to let future recruits know about this to attract them as part of their development and also to promote a culture that helps them do what they do best. The secret behind this is to leverage time off with remote work.

541. Using the 25% time off ideas to be presented as a speaker at events

Taking some of the big ideas generated and even implemented and using them as content at big events is a hook. This hook can be delivered as a speaker, ideally the growth hacker who came up with the big hack. This can be used to demonstrate to other growth hackers that there is research and development happening. The secret behind this is to attract the top minds, as they want to be part of it.

542. Using the 25% time off at a hacker house

Let your internal growth hackers take their time off at a hacker house, whether that be one you have sponsored, created or simply joined. This allows for new ideas to flow, and also for your growth hackers to network and identify new circuits from within the hacker house. The secret to this is sharing new ideas and getting them to take on the challenge with your team. This is a breeding ground to test out talent and get your next growth hacker onboard.

543. Using the 25% time off as part of your engagement on virtual coffee days

Use virtual coffee days to bring the new ideas generated in your 25% time off program. This helps your audience get attached to the development of new ideas, but also, when you bring your top decision-makers to the virtual coffee day, you create excitement and credibility. The secret behind this is to enable the audience to ask questions, build rapport, and more importantly to try even harder to be part of your organization.

544. Using the 25% time off ideas generated into growth hacking articles

Convert ideas generated in time off into articles. The secret here is you don't have to give away your best ideas. The point is creating content, and getting your audience engaged. In fact, this might be great grounds for inputs from your audience to improve your growth hacks. So not only do you develop an outreach content program, but also an engagement tool. Aside from this, you give recognition to your existing team, which is important.

555. Using the 25% time off to utilize growth hacking communities for ideas

Tap into growth hacking communities for idea generation, but also engagement. Formally engaging them is important, and letting them know their inputs will be recognized is very important. The secret behind this is to allow the best talent to surface and for your team to test them out. This is a low-friction approach, which can yield a very fruitful outcome.

556. Compensation for highly successful growth hacks

If a growth hacker and his or her team has hit a home run, let them benefit. Incentivize them with performance pay on top of their regular compensation. Be clear of rules, including targets and time frames and payouts as well. This form of bonus compensation incentivizes their talent, and that is attractive to new talent looking at your organization.

557. Rank top 10 recruiters by compensation

This is based on the highest performing growth hacker hired by the recruiter. Showcase your top ten recruiters whose recruits have performed well. The secret behind this is to let them comment and give some insights into how they got this great hire.

558. YouTube videos of the top secrets recruiters are using

Use recruitment secrets for growth hackers as videos. Use the video to recruit other recruiters in your network and theirs. These videos can be used to show the money-making opportunity for freelance recruiters and how to use those secrets for themselves. This is based on the highest performing growth hacker hired by the recruiter.

559. Promote your top recruiters on social media

Use social media to promote the tips, tricks and secrets used by your top recruiter based on the performance of their hires. The secret behind this is to attract more recruiters and document their approaches to be used later on as well.

560. Get top recruiters to motivate employees to recruit

Combine your internal and external referral programs to stimulate each other. By showing some of the tricks used by external recruiters for growth hackers internally, this might inspire and generate some new ideas on how they can get more talent on the team. Obviously, they would be compensated for doing this, and that would be the primary motive behind this. The secret behind this is to get qualified leads.

561. Invite top recruiters to an open coffee day

Get your best external recruiters to share their top method of how they got those top performing growth hackers to your organization. This is a great way to expose your top decision makers in this informal event to new ideas on how talent is acquired and retained. The secret behind this is to build a recruitment force to capture more ground quicker.

562. Give an award to your top external recruiters

Beyond massaging their egos as a rank, give awards. The secret is creating several categories so you have several different winners. This is a great learning ground for your internal team but, more importantly, a motivational drive for external recruiters to continue getting you the best growth hackers possible.

563. Send to conferences and events

Send your talent to events to learn but also to recruit. Incentivize this activity beyond just paying for the event and conference itself.

564. Live feedback on conferences and events

Broadcast the participation of your employees at conferences and events. News-jack their media and social media attention. The secret behind this is to use their handles, hashtags and anything else to leverage them. Keep plugging in to your content when covering a growth hacking hiring angel. Go one step further and register a member of the media and get access to the media center to gain even more coverage on your presence and give the message from within.

565. Post takeaways on conferences and events

Got some serious ideas or opinions based on conference content and agenda? Post it. Use their content and agenda to drive growth hacking positioning within your content. The secret behind this is to use this wisely to support others and leverage their reach.

566. Post meeting with key growth hackers at conferences and events

Use the power of FOMO (fear of missing out) by showing the ability to connect with some very cool people. The secret behind this is to enable you to show that one of the great opportunities of working as a growth hacker with your firm is getting these unique opportunities.

567. Blog the conferences and events

Write an article on your blog, send it out via your newsletter and put social media posts promoting it. The idea is to give a summary from a growth hacking perspective for those who did not join. The secret behind this is to use the media asset space to promote your hiring goals and, if you have a live position open, push it directly.

568. Vlog the conferences and events

Turn that blog post into a video blog post on YouTube. Same format, even the same content, but make it into a video. Capture moments within the event, including those unique connections. The secret behind this is that it is a way to drive interest from future growth hackers who want to be part of this sort of culture and get those benefits too.

569. Media center access

Have a member of your media/marketing team register as a member of media and cover the event on your blog or YouTube channel. Once you get your media agent inside, get them to network with other members of the media and push coverage of your company by introducing them on the spot to key contacts with stories ready to go. This needs preparation and media training for your team. The secret behind this is tapping into the media center to build media contacts and interest on the spot for your brand without it being very obvious.

570. Paid work vacations

Vacations are different but work vacations are a reality. They happen, and will continue to occur. So compensate for this. Allow them to do it, and to be fairly compensated as they blend their time and efforts.

571. Socialize those paid work vacations

Go viral, and get those amazing moments out there to incentivize your employees to do so. Position it as "the life of a growth hacker" as this helps boost interest. The secret behind this is to bring in new people; it helps get experienced growth hackers and may introduce the topic to new talent who want to enter it.

572. Bring the crew with you on those paid work vacations

Make this paid vacation a team thing. Take your growth team and have a paid getaway where you can show how growth teams work well together, even on the go. This again attracts both new and expected talent to the idea of a great workplace. Don't be shy to have a call to action for any who want to join the team. The secret behind this is to attract top talent through your work culture for growth hackers.

573. Invite potential hires on paid work vacations

Got a few high profile hires you want to make? Set up a small, low-cost paid vacation that is not too far away yet really cool. And yes, invite that high profile hire with you guys in a no-obligation and no-risk situation. The secret behind this is to allow for a chemistry check and it will be well worth it to show future growth hackers that they are important.

574. Take interns and apprentices on paid work vacations

Take your top interns and apprentices as a bonus. But don't just give this away, give it to top performers as a 'thank you', but also as a gateway to continue to attract and retain them on to the team full-time. The secret behind this is that this sort of investment pays off, both in the short and long term, and also galvanizes loyalty and high performance.

575. Let's go to a game, and get paid

Use the opportunity of the FIFA World Cup, the Superbowl or the like to get your team out there, paid by your organization. Get them wearing your t-shirts as well and, if possible, get them a behind-the-scenes walk-through. Give some sort of a value-add with visibility but one that's also fun for the team. Finally, have the team go live and post on social media as part of their outing. Having a good videographer help them might be worthwhile as part of your content in attracting future candidates. The secret behind this is leveraging popular games for your team to have fun and bond but at the same time creating a buzz around your hiring brand.

576. Communication hotspots

There are many under-utilized media assets to be used. Knowing them and using them will lower costs, widen your spread and help your brand.

577. *Dedicated growth hacker hiring landing page*

First and foremost is having a dedicated growth hacker hiring landing page. Yes, keep it unique with content related to your growth and growth hacking practice. At the same time, be open to hiring at any time, even if a position is not open. The secret behind this is to enable applicant tracking systems and be open about your work culture from a growth hacker's perspective.

578. Gamify your growth hacker hiring landing page

Find a way to engage your growth hackers. The secret behind this is to gamify their experience on your landing page to get them excited and share your dedicated hiring page.

579. Showcase growth cases on the growth hacker hiring landing page

Got some cool growth hacks? Feature them on your dedicated landing page and get your audience to engage. Ask for comments and reviews to generate even more ideas. Use this as an opportunity to generate new open ideas, but also to recruit and test talent. The secret behind this is awareness, and lead generation into your hiring funnel.

580. Calendar for coffee days on growth hacker hiring landing page

Promote your open coffee days, whether virtual or physical. Have a direct call to action to join future coffee days. Also, clearly promote the fact that your top decision makers and growth team will be there and that it is an opportunity to get to know them. The secret behind this is that it is about building trust and relationships, it's not a formal hiring process.

581. Internship program on growth hacker hiring landing page

Get your interns in and promote them. Use your dedicated growth hacker landing page to drive this and keep it active. The secret behind this is direct recruitment for entry-level positions into your organization.

582. Put your own events on the growth hacker hiring landing page

Develop your own events for attracting growth hackers. This can include hiring a top growth hacking instructor, mentor or coach and using this as a way to connect with future recruits. The secret behind this is to have a direct call to action and advertize featured events way in advance.

583. Sign-ups on growth hacker hiring landing page

Openly have a subscription call to action to get emails and names. It's simple and it works. The secret behind this is to build up your mailing list for direct and indirect recruitment opportunities.

584. Open referral program on growth hacker hiring landing page

Promote an open referral program and demonstrate payouts. The secret behind this is to incentivize people to open their networks within their audience.

585. Email signature

Use everyone's email signature to state that you're hiring. This is a virtual approach that makes use of having a link to your landing page and specific hiring page across the organization.

586. Link your YouTube video for recruitment

Place your YouTube Video link for general growth hacker recruitment. Keep this consistent and when you have a live hire, replace this with your open growth hacker position. The secret behind this is to generate leads into your hiring funnel.

587. Link live open positions

Place a live open position directly into your signature. State "We are hiring!" and then be specific that it is a growth hacker vacancy rather than a general position. The secret behind this is to keep top-of-mind.

588. Feature your dedicated growth hacker hiring page

Not actively hiring right now but want to remain passive? The secret behind this is to keep a dedicated link in your signatures to your dedicated growth hacker hiring page.

Let's hire the best talent

This exercise helps identify the best hacks to hire talent. This enables you to track performance, re-use top performers, discard poor performers, and create new hacks that might outperform existing ones. Choose hacks you want to use. Write down the number and name of the hack. Once a hack is applied, capture top-level learning points and the result.

Hack `#` Name of hacked

Learning What did you learn?

Result What are the results?

Hack `#` Name of hacked

Learning What did you learn?

Result What are the results?

Hack `#` Name of hacked

Learning What did you learn?

Result What are the results?

Hack `#` Name of hacked

Learning What did you learn?

Result What are the results?

Hack `#` Name of hacked

Learning What did you learn?

Result What are the results?

Performance of hacks

Capture, top, and poor performance hiring hacks here. At the same time, generate new hacks by combing existing hiring hacks or using existing hacks to inspire a new hiring hack. Use this performance page to develop your next action plan with your team to outperform your competition in finding, attracting, and retaining top growth talent.

Top performing Hacks

Hack | # | Name of hacked

Hack | # | Name of hacked

Hack | # | Name of hacked

Poor performing Hacks

Hack | # | Name of hacked

Hack | # | Name of hacked

Hack | # | Name of hacked

New Combo Hacks

Hack | # | Name of hacked | # | Name of hacked

Hack | # | Name of hacked | # | Name of hacked

Hack | # | Name of hacked | # | Name of hacked

New generated hacks

Hack | # | Name of hacked

Hack | # | Name of hacked

Hack | # | Name of hacked

589. Feature top performers in your signature

Feature your top performers. It's a bit like celebrating your employee of the month. However, tell it like a growth story. The secret behind this is to get people to tell others about this, and showing you're openly promoting your top talent positions your organization as a good place to work for growth hackers.

590. Feature your upcoming events and conferences

When making your own event, or joining one (virtual or physical), use this opportunity to gain traction with your direct contacts. Although this may be indirect in nature, it's a great way of warming up existing relationships and utilizing these opportunities for recruitment or recruitment referrals. The secret behind this is using it in a more direct response approach by stating you will have this event, and would like to meet new recruits, or be referred to new recruits, as an opportunity to meet them.

591. Email newsletter

Got a newsletter? Put in that you're hiring. Be specific and use your landing page and specific job page, if any. Use storytelling to draw attention to your hiring process for growth hackers. Don't forget to be growth hacker-oriented to attract them.

592. Link your chatbot to your newsletter

Always feature your hiring chatbot in your newsletter. Make it interesting with a story, and use the chatbot to ask questions about your growth hacking team and growth hacker positions. The secret behind this is to tap into your current audience to filter out direct and indirect recruitment opportunities.

593. Promote your social media posts in your newsletter

Repurpose your social media content into your newsletter. This way, you have more content and consistency in your newsletter. Use the social content used to promote working at your organization as a growth hacker in your newsletter. The secret behind this is, if you get interesting comments or questions, feature them in the newsletter.

594. Push your open positions in your newsletter

Don't be shy; when you have an actively open position, put it in your newsletter. In fact, pre-announce it to prepare your audience 2-3 weeks in advance. The secret behind this is, once you get built up, use this to promote the position and, more importantly, get your audience to share and recruit for you.

595. Get your dedicated growth hacker hiring page known

Keep a dedicated link in your ongoing newsletter for your growth hacking hiring dedicated landing page. The secret behind this is creating awareness and sustaining leads into your hiring funnel.

596. Highlight growth cases

Done something cool or got some serious results? Share this growth case in your newsletter to get growth hackers interested in your organization. The secret behind this is to attract top talent to the top challenges. Top minds are always attracted to top problems they want to solve.

597. Feature your interns in your newsletter

Highlight your top interns and allow them to get to know real people who want to aspire. This gives your audience motivation and a willingness to be part of your story. The secret behind this is stimulating recommendations, showing your support for talent and landing top recruits.

598. Promote your open referral payments program

Recruit the recruiters themselves. Directly promote your referral program in an open format, meaning get anyone to get paid for recruiting for you. The secret behind this is opening larger networks you cannot access and reaching into deeper corners you cannot see.

599. Feature your hacker house in your newsletter

Got a hacker house? Put the stories happening there into your newsletter. The secret behind this is letting your audience know that your hacker house is active and is actively recruiting growth hackers.

600. Recruit growth mentors and coaches via newsletter

Hire a growth mentor or coach weekly. Use your newsletter to recruit them but also to feature them to show your active participation in the growth hacking space. The secret behind this is attracting and placing top growth hackers in your organization.

601. Corporate social responsibility as a hiring strategy

'Help us hire someone, and we will give to a cause' or 'For every hire, we give to a cause' and 'Our new hotels contribute to this social cause'. The point is to link direct hires, or general hiring, to a social cause that is of interest to your audience, your firm and to the candidates you want to hire. The secret behind this is to link good intentions and deeds towards a cause people feel strongly about to your hiring process and practices. This can link either directly or indirectly to such campaigns. These campaigns are best run year-long and can evolve into different directions over time with their own marketing.

602. Email transactions

Transactional emails are a lost opportunity. These are your welcoming messages, or emails of thanks or even a receipt for an order email. Use those emails to state that you're hiring growth hackers and, again, point them toward your dedicated landing page. Ensure it's growth hacker-oriented so it's not seen as generic, then it won't be ignored.

603. Drop a YouTube video link in transactional emails

Put a link to a growth hacker recruitment video in your transactional emails. Do not forget to mention that you're hiring and keep this consistent and ongoing. When you have a specific position, change it at that time for that position; otherwise, keep it running all the time. The secret behind this is consistency for keeping top-of-mind.

604. Feature a top performer in transactional emails

Highlight your top-performing growth hackers as a way to gain attention to how great your workplace is for growth hackers. This is a great way to gain exposure but also to show how, as an organization, you celebrate the success of your growth hackers. The secret behind this is widening your network reach without exerting much effort.

605. Give a virtual coffee invitation in transactional emails

'Let's have a coffee.' Drop a direct invitation in your transactional emails for potential growth hackers to meet your top decision-makers. This is a great way to break the ice. Remember, this is also a great way to get someone who might know another great growth hacker to send this as a suggestion. The secret behind this is making it shareable so you can take it to your audience's network.

606. Feature your award-winners in transactional emails

Promote your awards and award-winners to show your top growth hackers. This shows how you celebrate talent; plus, it gives a call to action to suggest a growth hacker. The secret behind this is tapping into your audience's network.

607. Placement opportunities for recruitment in transactional emails

When you have a Registration, Notification, Confirmation, Feedback, or a Shopping cart abandonment, you have heightened attention. It would not be optimal to draw away from the purpose of the email, but rather, have your recruitment messaging as a secondary or third-level message. The secret behind this is tapping into heightened awareness and action-driven emails to gain attention and drive traffic to your active positions.

608. Recruiting growth hackers via social media

Social media is powerful and it enables you to tap into your audience's network. That is the whole idea, to go several degrees deeper than your direct reach to find hidden growth hacking talent.

609. Social media bios

Use your social media bios with direct links for hiring purposes. This doesn't have to be on all the time but, when you're actively hiring, this little but very variable piece can yield high returns quickly. The secret behind this is, of course, to send all traffic to your dedicated growth hacking landing page for recruitment.

610. Use your social bio to drive traffic to a job post

Put the job in your social bio. Simply grab social traffic straight into your job placement. This is a quick, easy and low-cost way to tap into your own audience. The secret behind this is creating referral programs as well; that helps you tap further into your audience's network.

611. Growth hacking group profile

Joining a growth hacking group? Design your profile effectively. Whether it be Facebook, LinkedIn or another platform, they will usually let you create your own profile. Use your logo for the image, and state that you have for a job opening. In the profile description, state the growth hacker position that's open and give it a deadline, even if it's an open application period. The secret behind this is tapping into the growth hacking community to unlock hidden talent.

612. Put your growth hacking demo day in your social media bio

Get your audience interested and watching your demo day. Use this also to recruit future growth hackers into your ecosystem. Do this by advertizing the demo day as an event for growth hackers only. The secret behind this is that it is directly tapping into growth hackers within the startup ecosystem.

613. Link your dedicated hiring page in your social media bios

It's simple. Get social traffic from your social networks directly onto your hiring page dedicated for growth hacker hires. The secret behind this is to brand and label it for growth hackers, so they know it's for them.

614. Feature award-winning growth hackers in your social media bio

You don't have to do this for a long period; even if it's for a single day, it can work well. Use this to massage the ego of the winners, and signal them to share this prestigious mention. Be sure to tell them it's for a limited time. The secret behind this is to put it on your internal landing page on your hiring site that features the winner but also using your chatbot or other mechanics to draw in future recruits.

615. Open coffee day announced on social media bio

That's right, announce the open coffee day (either physical or virtual) as an opportunity to meet your top leaders and your growth team. The secret behind this is that it's about conversation and rapport building, not formal interviews.

616. Hosting top growth hacking instructor in social media bio

Mention the top growth hacking instructor for people to sign up. Be clear that this is for growth hackers, so you get the growth-filtered audience in place. The secret behind this is to tap into other networks via your audience.

617. Social media posts

Use your social media posts to advertise your hiring program. Use content related to growth hacking and then attract those in the field by having a call to action to work for your organization. The secret behind this is to create value within the growth hacking community but it also shows you're open for business and want the top talent.

618. Show off paid work-vacations on social media

Get those watching jealous. That's right, send your growth hackers on working vacations in awesome places and post about it on social media. The secret behind this is to put a call to action, stating that if potential candidates want to live and work like this, they need to get recruited.

619. Highlight your apprentices on social media like a daily journey

Get your apprentices to share their learnings and outcomes for the day on social media and to tag and mention your company. The secret behind this is to show a day in the life of a growth hacker in the making.

620. Internship program on social media

Like the apprentice idea? Show-case your interns' lifestyle on a daily basis. Get them to post, share and attract others and to tag and mention your company's account.

621. Feature your top-performing hires on social media

Got a new hire doing well? Get him or her on social media and promote it. Use this as a way to show how your top talent is thriving and how great a workplace it is. Be sure they tag and mention your company account. The secret behind this is to promote top talent or attract more new talent.

622. Go live on social media for coffee

Make your coffee day go live on social media. Those who can join can perhaps send questions and be part of your coffee day virtually. The secret behind this is to collect the handles of those who do join and reach out afterwards via direct message to get them into your recruitment ecosystem.

623. Mentor or coach for hire as a social media post

Recruit the growth mentors and coaches via social media. Invite them for a mentor or coaching day and allow them to present their new ideas in growth hacking. The secret behind this is to present a paid opportunity for the top mentors and coaches from within. You can use them to develop your team but, more importantly, hire them or get them to hire for you.

624. Social media posts of growth challenge

Put your biggest challenges forward. Describe them well, put a structure in place, and let your audience know what you want them to solve. Give them a timeline, some tools and resources and a deadline. The secret behind this is it provides incentives to get the best talent solving your problems. This helps you solve problems directly but also enables you to hire top talent directly.

625. Leveraging the power of video

Leverage the power of video by engaging new audiences in a format they prefer. Using a combination of short- and long-form content can be very beneficial. A video is worth a million words. It tells a much deeper, richer and more engaging story than images or text alone. Video content is highly embraced, and growing at a very fast pace.

626. YouTube video

You have a few places to utilize this. One is the links in the video to draw traffic; the other is within the description itself and, of course, within the video content. Using this real estate allows you to draw on your cadence to help drive recruitment. The secret behind this is to give compensation for those who use their network to find you the right talent as well. You can also make a dedicated video or series of videos to hire growth hackers specifically.

627. YouTube video & reality apprentice show

If you make an apprentice program and decide to showcase it as a recruitment tool, use YouTube. YouTube is a great way to build an audience and attract talent via the content itself. The secret behind this is audience-building for direct and indirect recruitment purposes.

628. YouTube video & hiring affiliate program

Use YouTube to attract freelance recruiters into your affiliate program. This can be used as a way to present the opportunity and the specifics of hiring a growth hacker. The secret behind this is to arm your freelancer recruiters who are not on the payroll to do an amazing job of finding you the best talent.

629. YouTube video and creating your own hacker house

Use footage of people in your growth hacker house program to attract others to the hacker house. This is a pre-launch point to cultivate talent and then hire the best of the growth hackers in the hacker house. The secret behind this is to recruit and promote the hacker house and the benefits of it, including the possibility of landing a great growth hacking job.

630. Free YouTube video growth hacking courses

Use YouTube as a way to place and promote your free growth hacking courses. In fact, you can run them for free via YouTube by putting them as unlisted videos. You can push them to a mailing list which you can then send the videos for the course via email. The secret behind this is to track progress and build a relationship as well. You can also go 100% open and free, which is another strategy.

631. Streaming an award or recognition on YouTube as a virtual event

Turn your awards and any recognitions you're giving away into an event and stream it on YouTube. Save the video on your video list so future growth hackers you want to hire can see the previous ones. The secret behind this is to encourage those who have won to share the videos in the future. They can also drive traffic to the award-giving session to help you generate more awareness and recruitment leads.

632. YouTube interviews with top growth hacking instructors

Use this content in an interview format to tap into the instructors' community and others'. Use the credibility of the instructor and position your growth challenges as part of the questions to help you recruit those who can solve it. The secret behind this is recruitment as a call to action. Be very explicit, so people don't get confused. This is a growth hacker recruitment video.

633. Chatbots for recruiting growth hackers

Use chatbots to engage potential growth hackers via your website. This is a great way to streamline frequently asked questions, provide resources and, most importantly, get them to apply for a position on your growth team.

634. Chatbots

It's wise to use a dedicated chatbot for recruiting growth hackers. This allows you to address frequently asked questions quickly and effectively. The secret behind this is to generate leads passively without having to over-promote or invest. This is great for hiring a growth hacker.

635. Chatbots & YouTube video

Create a video about hiring growth hackers for your organization and link the video to a chatbot as a call to action for immediate interest. The secret behind this is to help generate leads quicker and at a lower cost.

636. Chatbots & social media posts

Use social media posts to drive traffic to your chatbot for hiring growth hackers. This is another quick and easy way to lower cost and increase leads generated for growth hacker positions. The secret behind this is lead generation, directly into your hiring funnel.

637. Chatbots & dedicated landing page

Have your chatbot directly traffic to your dedicated landing page for hiring growth hackers. The secret behind this is to ensure potential candidates know you have a dedicated growth hacking hiring page.

638. Chatbots & compensation for highly successful growth hacks

Use your chatbot to hire recruiters as well. Compensate them for recruiting high performance growth hackers for you. Just because they are not interested, doesn't mean they can't get you someone else who is good or even better than them. The secret behind this is presenting income generating business opportunities for recruiters.

639. Chatbots & sponsor a hacker house

Hire directly from the chatbot into your hacker house as an entry point to your fully-fledged recruitment program. The secret behind this is get potential recruits into an environment where you can test them, allow them to grow and, eventually, hire the best of them.

640. Chatbots & throw a party

Throwing a party at an event or a hacker house? Get those tapping into the chatbot to join in, physically or even virtually. The secret behind this is to get growth hackers to network with your team, to use informal hiring practices to get the best talent.

641. Chatbots & Starbucks credits giveaway

Use your chatbot to give away Starbucks coffee credits so they can join your team to get to know them. If there are virtual, do the same but have it also virtual at the same time. The secret behind this is to incentivize engagement.

642. Chatbots & apply for an award

Recruit positional growth hacking award winners via your chatbot. This is one step removed but it helps to cultivate future hires if you're not hiring right away. The secret behind this is to attract top talent you do not have on your radar.

643. Chatbots & demo days or competitions

Running demo days, or competitions, is a great way to push chat-bot leads into those channels as a way to test out the incoming tal-ent. The secret behind this is to tap into hidden talent.

644. Chatbots to growth hacker community

Build your own growth hacking community and get them to join via the chatbot as a way to springboard them into the recruitment process. The secret behind this is to attract potential talent and sup-port them to develop then, eventually, hire them directly.

645. Creativity unleashed

To attract new talent and appeal to a more dynamic and creative group of people, it is important to use creative means. Creative ac-tivities boost your employer branding, but also get your future re-cruits' creativity engaged early on in the process.

646. Create a song

Want to attract some younger, more dynamic growth hacking talent? Appeal to what they like by creating a song that will get their attention. The secret behind this is to boost your employer branding, popularize your song and attract younger, more dynamic growth hackers, especially at the entry level.

647. Create a song and outsource the process as an activity

Can't create an appealing song from within your team? Make the outsourcing process part of the creative process by engaging the community and tapping into upcoming artists. The secret behind this is tapping into upcoming artists who are willing to be very creative but who also can better relate to your target audience than you can.

648. Get others to remix the song

Got your song in place? Use popular services such as TikTok and other social media platforms to get others to remix your song. The secret behind this is to tap into a wider range of artists who can bring more appeal to your brand, and attract more recruits.

649. Get others to build on that song

Got your first song under your belt? Outsource again and get artists to make new songs along the same creative brief. The secret behind this is tapping into emotional triggers that stimulate your audience, such as their current struggles and/or interests. You don't want to be controversial so try to be tactful with your choices.

650. Get others to create new songs inspired by yours

Beyond building on your original brief, inspire others to create from scratch for you. This way, you can tap into more talent and attract newer growth hackers. The secret behind this is expanding on ideas, such as music that stimulates employees while working, or music that's meditative in nature, or even a playlist to support focus and motivation.

651. Create a music video

Take your initial song and turn it into user-generated music videos. TikTok and other social platforms are perfect for this sort of approach. The secret behind this is to run a challenge or competition to actively encourage others to create videos, but also to find inspiration in the song(s) and turn it into a visual story.

652. Pick the best video

Get others to make videos, and then pick the best and sponsor the creators to make it your office recruitment music video. The secret behind this is user-generated content and talent support. Not only do you get a relevant product at the end, but you will attract growth hackers by showing you're an organization that supports talent.

653. Get others to remix it

Got more than one video, or want to get very creative with the video content itself? Let users generate their own new creations using your existing videos. The secret behind this is to create more volume to continue to increase your reach but, more importantly, source the most popular music videos to promote and use them to bring in new talent.

654. Time to create a new song with a new video

Use the initial inspiration to create a whole new song and video. The secret behind this is tapping deeper into more creativity, but it also gives you more content to promote, and see what works best to attract new talent.

655. Use the music video in your recruitment channels

Use the most popular of your music videos in your formal recruitment channels and marketing. The secret behind this is to expand the creative talent into other applications for recruiting new talent.

656. Create a metaverse experience

Metaverse is emerging, and tapping into virtual reality experiences can be a great way of automating and engaging the talent among your younger audience. The secret behind this is to allow them to get a taste of the fun and creative side of working for your organization.

657. Metaverse - meet the CEO

Create a metaverse experience that involves your CEO in the experience. This gives an opportunity for new talent at all levels to take on a top-level executive role. This enables roleplaying for making hard decisions and dramatizing the experience to see what happens in extreme situations. The secret behind this is engagement, testing talent, and staying relevant.

658. Metaverse - meet the team

Get the team members an avatar on the metaverse and enable potential recruits to interact with future team members before even applying for a job. Of course, this is virtual and needs to be carefully curated. The secret behind this is to engage talent before applying and it's an opportunity to test them out in light situations.

659. Metaverse - intern for us

Don't have physical space? No worries! Use the metaverse to onboard many interns at once. This would be a light and low-touch experience but an interesting role-play opportunity to see how interns respond to various situations. The goal is to gamify this experience and finally win a real opportunity to join the internship program itself. The secret behind this is getting interested in more scalable matters for attracting, light testing and placing interns.

660. Metaverse - solve a real problem

Create a situation with extreme dynamics to make it entertaining. Use a real-world problem with real impact to see how well they perform. Use gamification to incentivize and drive performance in a virtual environment. The secret behind this is testing out talent with little investment in time, money and efforts for direct recruitment.

661. Create your own "why hire me?" videos

Streamline hiring by getting recruits to create a "hire me" video within guidelines set by you. It should ideally be no more than 60 seconds long, addressing 3 points and with a final conclusion. The secret behind this is seeing talent in action with little investment in time and money. This would be a great part of a hire funnel build-up, such as having a follow-up video for short-listed candidates.

Let's hire the best talent

This exercise helps identify the best hacks to hire talent. This enables you to track performance, re-use top performers, discard poor performers, and create new hacks that might outperform existing ones. Choose hacks you want to use. Write down the number and name of the hack. Once a hack is applied, capture top-level learning points and the result.

Hack [#] Name of hacked

Learning [ ] What did you learn?

Result [ ] What are the results?

Hack [#] Name of hacked

Learning [ ] What did you learn?

Result [ ] What are the results?

Hack [#] Name of hacked

Learning [ ] What did you learn?

Result [ ] What are the results?

Hack [#] Name of hacked

Learning [ ] What did you learn?

Result [ ] What are the results?

Hack [#] Name of hacked

Learning [ ] What did you learn?

Result [ ] What are the results?

Performance of hacks

Capture, top, and poor performance hiring hacks here. At the same time, generate new hacks by combing existing hiring hacks or using existing hacks to inspire a new hiring hack. Use this performance page to develop your next action plan with your team to outperform your competition in finding, attracting, and retaining top growth talent.

Top performing Hacks

Hack | # | Name of hacked

Hack | # | Name of hacked

Hack | # | Name of hacked

Poor performing Hacks

Hack | # | Name of hacked

Hack | # | Name of hacked

Hack | # | Name of hacked

New Combo Hacks

Hack | # | Name of hacked | # | Name of hacked

Hack | # | Name of hacked | # | Name of hacked

Hack | # | Name of hacked | # | Name of hacked

New generated hacks

Hack | # | Name of hacked

Hack | # | Name of hacked

Hack | # | Name of hacked

662. Hire me, here is why

Set up a campaign whereby those who qualify can send you a 60-second video on why they are a good hire. Keep this campaign open and ongoing to consistently have a feed of talent. The secret behind this is to filter well at the start and have a preset format for them to follow to make this process effective.

663. Hire me, solve a problem

Set up a campaign with key growth problems you're currently solving, and have qualified candidates give you a 30-second pitch. If you approve their pitch, invite them to give you a 2-minute video with the solution. Further filter, then request a 15-minute in-depth video going deeper. The secret behind this is using video as a funnel to qualify candidates through solving an existing growth problem.

664. Hire me, what the future will look like

Set up a video campaign about qualifying candidates in advance, then allow them to predict major changes in the growth space and why they are important. Create a video funnel; first is a 20-second pitch, then a 2-minute explainer, then a 15-minute in-depth talk. The secret behind this is to tap into future trends, and how growth hackers may tap into those trends and become part of your team.

665. Create a hiring game

Make hiring a fun experience! Create a game that is fun, challenging and reveals the data you need to determine whether a candidate is a good fit for your organization.

666. Problem-solving games

Create a game specifically around a growth hacking problem, such as how to acquire your first customer. The game needs to be simple, fun and easy for recruits to use. You also want it to be sharable, so others will want to participate. The secret behind this is to get young talent excited about the growth hacking challenges you will be putting in front of them, with the prospect of them landing a job.

667. Competitor battle games

Build a game with a simulated competitive landscape; this enables you to see how potential recruits will grow. This places them in the scenario of being in your organization and shows how they would handle competition. The secret behind this is that it is a great measure of competitive strategy and the candidate's ability to execute on it. Paired with a good gamification scoring system, this can become a vital part of your hiring funnel.

668. Role-playing your competitor to beat you

Flip the script! Turn future recruits into your competitors and get them to battle you for growth. This enables your organization to collect both competitive strategy data and also counter-competitive intelligence. The secret behind this is data collection and scoring systems to size-up potential recruits.

Order your copy of
Ready Set Growth Hack

https://www.amazon.com/Ready-Set-Growth-hack-beginners/dp/1916356915

Order your copy of
Growth Thinking Design

Conclusion

The conventional recruitment strategies that are currently used no longer yield the returns they once did. Technology, methodologies, and strategies have greatly advanced and, using the sciences of exponential growth, recruiters and heads of growth can effectively tap into growth talent using these 666+ dirty recruitment hacks.

The battle for growth talent is real, and it's getting fiercer by the day. Your competitors are most likely already tackling this problem and may have an advantage you haven't yet seen. The good news is that no one has entirely mastered this, due to the quickly shifting dynamics and a rapidly emerging discipline.

These 666+ dirtiest recruitment hacks are designed to give you an edge; an advantage that no one else can copy. To make that happen, you need to tailor these ideas to your organization, industry and geography. There is no single success formula and that is where the biggest opportunity is for bold, open-minded and growth-oriented organizations.

Use these dirty hacks wisely, and with good judgment.

About the author

*KNOWN AS **"the guy you never want your competition to hire"***

Nader Sabry is a keynote speaker, strategist, innovator, and entrepreneur as well as a leading voice in innovation, space technology, government, and health/wellness. He is a passionate advocate for inspiring young people to embrace science and technology, through the Get2space.com initiative in partnership with the US Space Foundation.

Sabry has directly raised US $20 million in venture capital, $100 million indirectly for startups he has advised or cofounded, and $3 billion in foreign direct investment. He was the 43rd person in history to be NASA Space Technology certified, has served as a judge for the US Space Foundation's Space Technology Hall of Fame, is a top-50 writer globally on medium.com, has been ranked one of the top 13 innovators in the MENA region making a difference in Step Conference, and was featured by Kearney Global Management Consultancy as one of their top alumni.

Sabry is the former CEO and Founder of TIMEZ5 Global Inc., a Canadian space technology company certified by NASA's Space Foundation, and a GIES Innovation award-winner from His Highness Sheikh Mohammed Bin Rashid Al Maktoum. TIMEZ5 was founded in 2012 after five years of R&D selling in 37 countries; it has been recommended by healthcare professionals globally.

Prior to TIMEZ5 Global, Sabry was head of innovation and thought leadership at Kearney, chief strategist for The Dubai Department of Economic Development, and director of strategy for the Dubai Foreign Investment Office. He has also advised several governments and Fortune 1000 companies.

HIRE ME IF YOU CAN

HIRE ME IF YOU CAN

www.ingramcontent.com/pod-product-compliance
Lightning Source LLC
Chambersburg PA
CBHW041207220326
41597CB00030BA/5084